DISTANCE EDUCATION
A PRACTICAL GUIDE

DISTANCE EDUCATION
A PRACTICAL GUIDE

BARRY WILLIS
University of Alaska

EDUCATIONAL TECHNOLOGY PUBLICATIONS
ENGLEWOOD CLIFFS, NEW JERSEY 07632

Library of Congress Cataloging-in-Publication Data

Willis, Barry.
  Distance education : a practical guide / Barry Willis.
    p. cm.
  Includes bibliographical references and index.
  ISBN 0-87778-255-5
  1. Distance education—Handbooks, manuals, etc. I. Title.
LC5800.W55 1993
371.3'078—dc20   92-32544
                                                      CIP

Printed in the United States of America.

Library of Congress Catalog Card Number: 92-32544.

International Standard Book Number: 0-87778-255-5.

First Printing: January, 1993.

Contents

Preface

This resource is designed as a practical guide and reference tool for faculty and administrators seeking to plan, develop, and implement effective distance education programs and learning materials.

Faculty will find historical information, summaries of comparative research in the field, the roles and responsibilities of those involved in distance education, and a step-by-step process for designing, developing, evaluating, and revising instruction for delivery at a distance. Other chapters discuss the teaching tools and technology of distance education and practical strategies for maximizing their strengths while minimizing their inherent weaknesses.

Administrators will find information on the evolution of distance education and strategies for the design, creation, implementation, and administration of in-service training programs. Also included is a discussion of the academic policy issues and organizational challenges to be addressed in effectively delivering instruction at a distance.

Effective distance education programs don't just happen; they evolve as the result of systematic planning and a detailed understanding of the individual needs and diverse characteristics of the distant learners they are intended to serve. While few would dispute the critical role played by technology in this evolutionary process, technology alone is not "the answer." In fact, personal contact and face-to-face interaction remain critical components of many successful distance education programs. Taking this one step further, it is the author's belief that the role and importance of personal contact and face-to-face interaction will actually increase as educators gain familiarity with the challenges of effective distance teaching.

In developing this book, several individuals provided advice and counsel. Reviewers included Stevan DeSoer, George Christensen, Barbara Bennett, Deborah Mercy, Susan Mitchell, Paula Elmes, and Regina Cockerill. Their comments, as well as the input of others, are gratefully acknowledged.

Barry Willis
Lake Clark, Alaska
July 1992

DISTANCE EDUCATION
A PRACTICAL GUIDE

1.0

Distance Education: Introduction and Overview

1.1 Introduction

The field of distance education has evolved worldwide over the past 10 years. As this evolution has unfolded, different phrases have been coined to describe the organizational framework and anticipated instructional outcomes that result. Phrases including "distance education," "distance learning," "distant teaching," "tele-work," "tele-learning," "outreach," and "tele-teaching" have been used to describe the same basic process and outcomes.

For consistency, "distance education" will be used here to describe the organizational framework and process of providing education at a distance. The phrase "distance learning" will be used to identify the intended instructional outcome, i.e., learning that takes place at a distance.

While distance education can solve many academic problems, it typically creates more than a few in the process.

In resolving the problems that are sure to arise, the educator's goal is clear: to capitalize on the strengths and capabilities offered by the distance delivery of

3

instruction while minimizing or eliminating the potential problems arising from its use.

This is the challenge of distance education and the focus of this resource. This book was developed to serve educators and administrators in two ways:

- To provide a practical foundation for planning, developing, and implementing effective distance education programs.
- To offer suggestions, advice, and encouragement for those accepting the challenge offered by this potentially effective form of instructional delivery.

1.2 An Overview of Distance Education

1.2.1 What is distance education? At its most basic level, distance education takes place when a teacher and student(s) are separated by physical distance, and technology (i.e., voice, video, data, and print) is used to bridge the instructional gap.

To be effective, the technology of distance education should remain relatively transparent, allowing the instructor and students to concentrate on the process of teaching and learning.

Unfortunately, due to the captivating nature of many distance delivery technologies and techniques, faculty, students, and administrators can easily become distracted by the opportunities and limitations of the delivery system and lose sight of the academic needs to be met. In fact, if faculty, staff, and students are constantly being reminded of the technological delivery system itself, either through technical problems or through impressive but unnecessary technological capabilities, they will be distracted from effective teaching and learning.

For this reason, it is critical for the distant educator to remain firmly focused on instructional goals, content requirements, student needs, and delivery constraints.

Still, it's easy to get bogged down with the notion of distance and falsely assume that bridging relatively long distances requires more planning and effort than teaching over short distances. Although this makes sense initially, further investigation leads to the realization that the same challenges must be faced and difficulties overcome whether students are two blocks, two miles, or two time zones away.

In fact, whether the course is delivered face-to-face or at a distance, critical instructional elements remain unchanged. These include organizing, planning, understanding student needs and characteristics, developing content, and gaining familiarity with presentation methods.

1.2.2 How do you plan and implement an effective distance education program? Without exception, effective distance education programs begin with careful planning and an understanding of course requirements and student needs. Appropriate technology can only be selected once these elements are understood in detail.

There is nothing magical about effective distance education programs. They don't just happen; they are planned with an attention to detail often exceeding that required in traditional, face-to-face teaching.

Seldom is an effective distance education course a one-person operation. A fully functioning distance education effort requires the consistent and coordinated work of administrators, faculty, on-site facilitators, technicians, and support personnel.

While each individual plays a different role, they have a common goal: to provide relevant and well-planned distance learning experiences to a select group of learners.

1.2.3 What's the difference between distance-delivered instruction and face-to-face teaching?

Whether they realize it or not, effective classroom teachers rely on a number of visual and unobtrusive cues and clues from their students. A quick glance, for example, reveals who is attentively taking notes, pondering a difficult concept, or enthusiastically preparing to make a comment. The student who is frustrated, confused, tired, or bored is equally evident. The attentive teacher consciously and subconsciously receives and analyzes these visual cues. As a result, the delivery of information, and often the course content itself, is adapted to meet the unique characteristics and needs of the class during any particular lesson.

The student coming to class with organized class notes, a well-used text, and obvious enthusiasm reveals something quite different from the withdrawn student arriving without class materials or a receptive attitude. Again, alert face-to-face teachers factor these unobtrusive cues into their class planning and delivery.

A traditional classroom setting offers the teacher and students many opportunities for interaction outside of class. Maybe they talk between classes, meet on a class assignment over lunch, or have mutual interests. Just living in the same community provides a common frame of reference that leads to understanding and familiarity.

Finally, face-to-face interaction takes place without any technological linkage. Communication is free flowing and spontaneous, without the need to manipulate switches, ignore static, look into a camera, or rely on a piece of technical equipment linking teacher and students for purposes of communication and feedback.

In contrast, distant teachers have few, if any, visual cues. Even the visual cues that do exist are filtered through technological devices such as video monitors. The effortless flow of a stimulating teacher-class conversation can feel contrived when spontaneity is altered by technical requirements and distance.

Without the use of a real-time visual medium such as television, the teacher receives no visual information from the distant sites. The teacher never really knows if, for example, students are asleep, talking among themselves, or even in the room. Separation by distance also affects the general rapport of the class. Living in different communities, geographic regions, or even states deprives the teacher and students of a common community link.

Until the faculty member becomes familiar with the delivery technologies being used, there is vague discomfort that the instructional message is not coming across as intended, or that the technology is reducing the effectiveness of the course for teacher and students alike.

1.2.4 Given the inherent challenges and potential difficulties, why teach at a distance? By any measure, teaching at a distance is challenging. Whether the challenges are worth confronting depends on the instructional mission of the institution, the nature of the content, the faculty's desire and ability to adapt their teaching styles, the characteristics of the students, the time available for planning, the technical systems to be used, and the support service infrastructure.

Still, the challenges inherent in distance teaching are accompanied by opportunities to reach a wider student audience; to meet the needs of students who are unable to attend on-campus classes; to link students from different social, cultural, economic, and experiential backgrounds; and to include speakers from different parts of the state, country, or world who would be unable to attend a traditional session (see Henderson & Nathenson, 1984).

There is no denying that distance education is challenging to both faculty and students. It presents obstacles to overcome and logistical concerns to address. Still, many feel the opportunities offered by distance education outweigh the obstacles. In fact many instructors feel that the experience of teaching at a distance improves their overall teaching ability and empathy for their students.

1.3 The International Roots of Distance Education

In distant education, as in other endeavors, it's difficult to know where you're going if you don't know where you've been.

Despite the higher visibility it has received in the past several years, distance education has been around a long time and is a direct outgrowth of earlier print-based correspondence study programs. In the United States, the historical roots of present-day distance education can be traced to the early 1700s, when advertisements first appeared for courses offered by mail and labeled "correspondence study." In the early 1800s, public lectures in rented facilities became popular as an outgrowth of the Greek Lyceum (the grove of trees in Athens where Aristotle taught), and by

1835 there were more than 3,000 Lyceum halls in 15 states. By the 1870s, correspondence courses, offered by mail, gained international popularity, with courses offered in many countries, including Sweden, England, Germany, Canada, as well as the United States (Ohler, 1988).

By the early 1900s, correspondence study was flourishing with universities and private schools providing instruction to elementary, secondary, higher education, and vocationally-oriented learners.

The visibility of distance education programs combining print and non-print resources received a boost in 1969 when the Open University of the United Kingdom was established and began to systematically develop and deliver integrated distance education programs. This was followed in the early 70s with the start-up of Canada's Athabasca University, an institution expressly created to research and provide distance-learning opportunities through the combined use of innovative technology and traditional home-study techniques.

Since the early 1970s, the British influence has been dominant in distance education, with England, Canada, and Australia playing critical leadership roles on an international basis through various organizational structures, including the Open Learning Institute of British Columbia, the BC Knowledge Network, the Alberta Educational Communications Corporation, the University of Queensland Australia, and the University of Quebec.

In the United States, progress has been slower. While print-based correspondence study programs flourished, attempts to incorporate voice, video, and data technology proceeded sluggishly throughout the 1960s and early 70s. By the 1980s, however, many states found themselves heavily involved in the planning and implementation of innovative distance education programs (see Lewis, 1985).

With the 1989 publication of *Linking for Learning: A New Course for Education*, by the U.S. Congress, Office of Technology Assessment, came the realization that distance education initiatives were becoming widespread throughout the United States. At the present time, emphasis is shifting from single-technology delivery systems to integrated approaches seeking to cost-effectively combine voice, video, and data technology, often in tandem with print.

1.4 In Summary

The role and influence of distance education is currently in a period of evolutionary growth. Early efforts in the field focused on print-based correspondence study courses and single-technology approaches to instructional delivery with few opportunities for teacher-to-student and student-to-student interaction. In contrast, recent trends seek to innovatively integrate the unique characteristics of various voice, video, data, and print delivery systems.

2.0
Research in Distance Learning: Factors Enhancing Effectiveness

2.1 Summarizing Distance Learning Research

As in many educational fields, what we don't know about distance learning exceeds what we do know about it. Still, researchers have attempted to dissect and research the constituent parts of the distance learning process by exploring numerous variables, including student demographics, motivation, attrition, cognitive style, gender, and achievement.

Sponder (1990) summarized research findings, focusing on many of these variables. Another comprehensive research summary explored various components of the distance learning process (see Moore & Thompson, 1990). Areas summarized in this study include:

- *Effectiveness of distance learning.* Numerous studies have been conducted to explore the comparative effectiveness of distance and traditionally delivered instruction (Eiserman & Williams, 1987). The majority of studies concluded that distance-delivered instruction could be as effective as traditional

11

instruction if the delivery methods were selected based on:

* background and experience level of the student,
* cognitive style of the learner (see Nelson, 1985),
* diversity of students participating in the course, and
* appropriateness of the content being delivered.

Many studies concluded that the degree of teacher-student and student-student interaction and the selection of appropriate content examples were far more critical than the delivery system itself.

This suggests that content examples must be focused and relevant to individual learners. While mass media instructional approaches such as telecourses can be effective if students share common experiential backgrounds, students from diverse educational and cultural backgrounds may require more individualized approaches to instructional delivery.

* *Learner attitudes and perceptions.* Many studies conclude that adult attitudes toward distance delivery are positive (Boswell, Mocker, & Hamlin, 1968; Christopher, 1982; Hoyt & Frye, 1972).
* *Communication strategies.* While some studies indicate that distance delivery does not preclude effective communication and interaction (Smeltzer, 1986), other studies suggest that communication effectiveness is enhanced in face-to-face instruction when compared to distance-delivered course experiences. In terms of student attitudes, Davis (1984) found this to be especially true as the number of face-to-face interactions increased.
* *Program design, development, and evaluation.* A number of studies have suggested that distance delivery requires enhanced planning and manage-

ment skills on the part of faculty and support staff (Batey & Cowell, 1986). This same study suggests that effective distance education program planning requires a rigorous and systematic approach to development that is more prevalent in corporate training environments than higher-education settings.

Many studies indicate that teachers often have a more limited role in designing distance-delivered courses than in designing courses for traditional classroom delivery. Downing (1984) noted potential problems in removing the teacher from the course development process. These concerns are echoed by others who feel that course ownership must reside with the instructor, not the instructional developer. This suggests that the role of the developer is one of assistance not of control.

There is also wide agreement regarding the importance of formative and summative evaluation in distance education and the need to adapt traditional evaluation methods to the distance-delivery environment.

- *Cost-effectiveness of distance education.* Studies analyzing the cost-effectiveness of distance education typically compare such factors as transportation costs, savings in travel and preparation time, and potential enrollment increases. While the majority of studies in higher education settings suggests that distance delivery can be more cost-effective than transporting students to on-site instructional locations (Christopher, 1982; Showalter, 1983), many studies fail to take into account continuing personnel costs and the financial implications of developing and maintaining the required technical infrastructure.

While distance education may be cost-effective, it is never inexpensive.

2.2 Is There a "Best" Technology?

While distance education research has been varied and broad in focus, one area has received continuing interest since the instructional use of voice, video, and data technology first began. This has been the elusive search for the best technology and most effective delivery system.

Since the 1950s when B. F. Skinner experimented with the use of rudimentary teaching machines, educational researchers have attempted to evaluate the relative effectiveness of various technological delivery systems. Typically, these studies have been based on the assumption that the vehicle of instructional delivery (i.e., technology), was as important, if not more important, than the instructional content itself. Without questioning this assumption, numerous studies were conducted in the 1970s and 80s seeking to identify the best medium of instruction. Early research typically showed notable short-term performance gains whenever a new technology was compared with an established delivery tool.

In a meta-analysis of computer experiments, for example, Clark (1985) found that short-term gains usually resulted from the novelty of the new technology being used and had little to do with the attributes of the technology itself. In fact, comparisons of the long-term effects (i.e., over six months) of virtually every combination of voice, video, and data technology have been completed with the same typical result: no significant difference. Similar findings result when technological delivery systems are compared with traditional face-to-face approaches to instructional delivery.

In terms of instructional television, Verduin and Clark (1991) summarized the results of several important studies. Zigerell (1984) reviewed research comparing televised instruction with traditional face-to-face delivery and concluded that few performance differences could be found in equivalent courses.

In another research effort, Purdy (1978) reviewed studies of telecourse effectiveness including those conducted by the Chicago TV College, the Coast Community College District, and the University of Mid-America, and found few performance differences. Using a similiar strategy, Whittington (1987) reviewed over 100 studies comparing telecourse and conventional achievement. The majority of these studies reported equal or superior cognitive performance by telecourse students.

Chu and Schramm (1975) focused more broadly on television-based instruction. In doing so, they reviewed the vast majority of available studies at all academic levels that compared traditional classroom performance with television instruction in equivalent courses. As a result of this review, they concluded that a wide array of different courses had been successfully taught using television, with no significant difference in performance, when compared to more traditional methods of instructional delivery.

On occasion, some instructional television promoters have used the results of these studies to make the argument that instructional television is just as effective, in terms of student performance, as face-to-face delivery and is more cost-effective, especially when compared to the expense of rural instructional delivery.

These same proponents, however, downplay research completed in the 1970s that also found correspondence study courses to be as effective as face-to-face instruction. Macken (1976), for example, surveyed 67 American studies that explored correspondence education effectiveness at the college, technical, and high-school level and found no significant difference in learner outcomes between correspondence and conventional face-to-face instruction.

As reported in Verduin and Clark (1991), similar findings resulted from comparative studies of computer-based and conventional face-to-face instruction. Orlansky and String (1979) reviewed 48 studies of computer-based instruction in military settings and found it significantly superior in 15 of 48 comparisons. These researchers concluded that the overall difference in achievement had little practical significance due to the fact that no significant achievement differences were found in 32 studies. They did, however, find an additional savings of 30 percent in instructional time, as did Kulik, Kulik, and Schwalb in 1985.

2.3 Why No Performance Difference?

Finding no significant difference between technology-based and conventional face-to-face instruction should come as no surprise. Consider, for example, the following:

• Is a computer-based word processor instructionally more effective than a manual typewriter?
• Is the pencil an instructionally more effective writing tool than the pen?

Of course not. This is because distance-delivery technology, whether it be television, computer, or pencil, is a mere vehicle or medium of delivery and has little influence over student performance, as long as its characteristics are appropriate to the task at hand, and the *instructional design* is effective.

For example, if you are teaching someone to discriminate between various colors, the delivery technology must be capable of realistically illustrating different colors. You can't teach the color wheel via audioconferencing or black-and-white television. In this case the ability to show color is a needed characteristic of the delivery system. Similar logic suggests that teaching *movement* requires a delivery system that includes motion as a media characteristic.

The goal is to select instructional technology based on the media characteristics (e.g., sound, motion, etc.) required to effectively deliver the instructional content to the intended audience.

2.4 What Factors Impact Instructional Effectiveness?

If the characteristics of the delivery system are important only to the extent that they are appropriate to the content being presented, what factors *do* determine the effectiveness of distance learning?

Over the past several years, research exploring effective distance teaching efforts as well as evaluations of student attitude towards the use of distant delivery methods have resulted in some fairly consistent conclusions. These conclusions are worth considering when planning and implementing distance education programs, especially for rural and/or culturally diverse learners.

2.4.1 Teaching at a Distance Can Be Effective. If teaching techniques and delivery methods take into account the needs, diversity, and context of distance learners, teaching at a distance can be effective.

2.4.2 Select Contextually Relevant Examples. Instruction is presented through the use of content examples. These content examples must be relevant to the intended audience. This is often difficult for teachers who have little background and experience with the learners they'll be teaching.

Instructors tend to teach using the same examples that were used when they received their training. For distance learning to be effective, however, instructors must discover examples that are relevant to their distant students. A related strategy is to encourage students to find or develop locally relevant examples illustrating the points made in the course.

2.4.3 Understand Urban and Rural Students. Many students have similar backgrounds and a common frame of reference. This enables the instructor to use "mass media" instructional approaches and technologies such as prepackaged telecourses that capitalize on this common background. In contrast, many urban and rural learners, especially those with multicultural backgrounds, have unique and diverse characteristics that must be understood by the distant teacher (see Forbes, Ashworth, Lonner, & Kasprzyk, 1984). Meeting the needs of these students typically requires a more targeted instructional and technological approach that enables the instructor to individualize distance teaching strategies to meet the specific needs of these diverse learners.

2.4.4 Realize Family Support Is Critical. Distant students typically balance many responsibilities, including employment and raising children. Often their involvement in distance learning is unknown to those they work with locally, and ignored by family members at home. Student performance is enhanced if learners set time aside for their instructional activities and if they receive family support in their academic endeavors.

2.4.5 Establish Suitable Learning Environments. Distance learning is enhanced when local facilities are available for class and study. These facilities should include adequate learning resources (voice, video, and data technologies) and a communal learning environment.

2.4.6 Provide Timely Feedback. Timely and informative feedback is essential. It is critical for teachers to respond to students' questions, assignments, and concerns in a personalized and pleasant manner, using appropriate technology such as fax, phone, or computer. Informative comments that elaborate on the individual student's performance and suggest areas for improvement are especially helpful.

2.4.7 Encourage Student-to-Student Interaction. Students often learn most effectively when they have the opportunity to interact with other students. Interaction among students typically leads to group problem solving and should be encouraged. When students are unable to meet together, appropriate interactive technology such as electronic mail should be provided to encourage small group and individual communication. Consider assignments in which students work together and then report back or present to the class as a whole.

If multiple students reside in the same community, every effort should be made to have them participate as a class as often as possible. This group interaction is critical, even if available technology permits individual participation from home.

2.4.8 Enhance Student Motivation. High student motivation is required to complete distant courses because the day-to-day contact with teachers and other students is typically lacking. Instructors can help to motivate students by providing consistent and timely feedback, encouraging discussion among students, being well prepared for class, and by encouraging and reinforcing effective student study habits.

2.4.9 Foster Face-to-Face Contact. Distance delivery is no replacement for in-person contact. If possible, teach from distant sites early in the course and then meet individually with students. If this is impossible, arrange to meet with students when other business brings them to your community or vice versa.

2.4.10 Provide On-Site Facilitation. An on-site facilitator can be an effective bridge linking teacher and students (see section 3.4). While a facilitator with content expertise is especially valuable, even non-content facilitation can help the instructor gain a better understanding of the students and develop more responsive instruction. This is especially critical when urban instructors teach rural or multicultural students.

2.4.11 Reduce Attrition. Student attrition is typically higher in distance-delivered courses than in on-site instruction. This is the result of various factors, including limited student advising and counseling, poor family support, inadequate feedback, late return of assignments, and lack of personalized teacher-student and student-student interaction. The best way to reduce attrition is to treat each student as an individual, communicate with them often, and assist in establishing local or regional student support networks.

2.4.12 Help Students Keep Up with Assignments. Unclear performance expectations and a failure to keep up with assignments early in a course is a primary cause of student attrition. Providing adequate time to complete assignments and making performance standards explicit, especially early in a course, will discourage students from falling behind.

2.4.13 Put Time into Course Adaptation. Even a course taught repeatedly in a traditional format will typically require significant adaptation for delivery at a distance. The same is true for newly developed courses and is especially apparent when the course will be delivered to a new student population, whether rural or urban. Putting adequate time into course development and adaptation will make the course more relevant to distant learners and will, in the long run, be less time consuming and more rewarding for the instructor.

2.4.14 Provide Advising and Counseling Support. As with traditionally delivered instruction, advising and counseling is critical for the distant learner. The distances involved and the lack of common experiences among counselors and students makes the task of providing effective advising and counseling even more challenging. To enhance advising and counseling at a distance, consider using a toll-free phone number before, during, and after the course has been completed.

2.4.15 Be Sensitive to Hearing Problems. Distance learning is often critically dependent on a student's hearing ability. Unfortunately, hearing problems typically go undiagnosed. Occasionally, both in and outside of class, ask students if they can hear clearly and make arrangements for hearing tests where potential difficulties exist.

2.4.16 Deal Directly with Technical Problems. Regardless of the technology being used, technical problems will occur. Discuss potential problems and solutions with students prior to the start of class. Focus on joint problem solving, not placing blame for the occasional technical difficulty.

2.4.17 Provide Hands-on Training for Faculty. In-service training by faculty on the technical equipment used in the course (audioconferencing, television, computing, etc.) is essential. This training should be practical in nature and include hands-on experiences.

In addition, it is important for faculty to understand the roles being played by other team members, such as control room personnel (directors, camera operators) and support service staff (materials duplication and distribution personnel).

2.5 In Summary

Research suggests that effective distance learning is more the result of preparation than innovation.

The research suggests, for example, that distance education and traditionally delivered instruction can be equally effective if the distance educator puts adequate preparation into understanding the needs of the student and adapting the instruction accordingly. As with all forms of instruction, a teacher's understanding of the target population and their instructional needs is equally as important as mastery of the content being delivered.

An important part of this preparation is finding content-related examples that are relevant to the distant student. While this can be time consuming, the literature suggests it is critical. An outgrowth of this finding suggests that culturally diverse learners may require more individualized delivery approaches that take into account their cultural backgrounds and past life experiences.

As for delivery systems, the research suggests that there is no significant difference in the effectiveness of the delivery systems used, as long as the characteristics of the delivery system match content requirements. In other words, the content being presented and the capabilities of the delivery system must be complementary. A visual delivery system, for example, is needed to teach visual concepts.

While more research is needed, especially in multi-cultural settings, a fairly solid research foundation has been developed, leading to the conclusion that teaching at a distance can be effective.

3.0
The Key Players in Distance Education

3.1 Who Are the Key Players in Distance Education and What Are Their Roles?

To be effective, distance education requires the integrated efforts of several participants, including students, faculty, facilitators, support staff, and administrators. When effectively integrated, each brings a unique capability to the distance education enterprise. Similarly, the absence or under-involvement of a critical participant can dilute or derail the integrated efforts of other contributors.

This chapter highlights the unique roles filled by the principal distance education participants and explores the inter-relationships bringing them together.

3.2 Students

Meeting the instructional needs of students is the cornerstone of distance education, and the test by which all efforts in the field are judged. Ironically, some educators mistakenly assume that student needs are either self-evident or that others can make related decisions without a clear understanding of the needs and constraints faced by the target audience.

Regardless of the instructional context, the primary role of the student is to learn. Under the best of circumstances, this challenging task requires motivation, planning, and the ability to analyze and apply the information being taught. In a distance education setting, the process of student learning is made more complex for several reasons. The following identifies these complexities and then discusses strategies for addressing them.

3.2.1 Students are often separated from others sharing their backgrounds and interests. Learning is a dynamic process, with communication and interaction the principal forces behind this dynamism. Much has been written about the need and importance of two-way communication among distant students (Holmberg, 1985, 1990). A recurring theme is the nature of student-to-student interaction and the belief that communication among learners is critical to understanding and applying information.

Students, for example, often discuss course material with other students, even if uncomfortable doing so with the instructor. This is especially true for single student sites, although it is of concern in all distance education settings.

To facilitate student-to-student interaction, begin with some light conversation to make students comfortable with using the delivery technology. You can, for example, ask non-content questions regarding community life, recent events, or other topics to encourage informal conversation. Another possibility is to have each student distribute a biographical sketch for informal discussion during the first class session.

3.2.2 Students often begin class ill at ease with the instructor. Over time, as the teacher and students grow increasingly familiar, this uneasiness fades. Because distant teachers and their students often have little in common in terms of culture and day-to-day experiences, this familiarity can take longer to develop.

To increase the teacher-student comfort level, learn as much as possible about the students being taught. This information gathering should go beyond the content preparation of the student and include their cultural, social, and geographical background and interests.

The fastest way to eliminate uneasiness in a distance-delivered class is to contact local sites or individual students prior to the start of class and get to know them as individuals, not just students. If possible, visit participating sites in person. In addition to talking to the students themselves, talk with colleagues familiar with the distant sites, and local K–12 teachers.

3.2.3 In distance education settings, technology is typically the conduit through which information and communication flow. As a result, the student is expected to learn new information, from a new instructor, through a new method of communication, often in isolation, without the assistance and support of fellow students. No wonder distance learning is mysterious and imposing to many students.

Until the teacher and students become comfortable with the technical delivery system, communication will be inhibited. Practice is the best and fastest way to overcome these equipment-related communication obstacles.

In summary, students must be motivated, prepared for class, willing to ask questions, familiar with the delivery systems in use, and encouraged and supported by teachers, parents, and fellow students. Making strides in these areas will increase the amount of learning that takes place and the satisfaction the student receives in the process.

3.3 Faculty

To a great extent, the success of any distance education effort rests squarely on the shoulders of the faculty. Typically, however, faculty are not consulted when the configuration of the technical or support service infrastructure is being debated.

In a traditional classroom setting, the instructor's responsibility includes assembling course content and developing an understanding of unique student needs. Since content is taught through the use of examples, the teacher is expected to develop relevant content examples. This can be challenging because the content-related examples the instructor learns in preparatory training are sometimes difficult to separate from the content itself.

The effective teacher constantly monitors class progress and modifies content delivery as well as the examples being used. While this is difficult in traditional settings, special challenges confront those teaching at a distance:

3.3.1 The instructor must develop an under-standing and appreciation for the characteristics and needs of students with little first-hand experience. Often, the student's realm of experience, living conditions, and culture are foreign to the instructor. To be effective, the instructor must understand the students, either through first-hand observation or through discussion with colleagues experienced with the targeted learner group. This step is critical if the instructor hopes to understand individual learners.

3.3.2 Although many instructors incorporate media and technology in their courses, the distance delivery instructor often relies on technology as the principal link with students. This requires familiarity with the strengths and weaknesses of the different delivery systems, and an ability to use them effectively in various instructional situations.

3.3.3 Most effective teachers consciously and subconsciously adapt their course content, delivery methods, and pacing as the class progresses. In traditional classroom settings, instructors can visually determine who is interested and involved and who isn't. In a distance delivery context, where technology is the primary link between teacher and student, this task is more difficult and time consuming. Rather than rely on subconscious cues as the course progresses, the instructor must go to extraordinary lengths to elicit feedback from and about students. This may require extra phone calls, individual student conferences, and contact with on-site facilitators and others who understand the needs of the participating students.

3.3.4 It takes time to develop or adapt a course for distance delivery. Instructors, especially those new to distance delivery, will be more effective if they realize up front that this method of teaching requires added instructional development time and effort. More time, for example, is needed to gain an understanding and appreciation of the participating students, to adapt content examples, and to master effective use of the technical delivery system. The distance-delivered course should not be viewed as just another teaching assignment.

3.3.5 The effective distance educator becomes a skilled facilitator in addition to being the primary content provider. Many different instructional elements must be effectively orchestrated by the distant educator. These include the content being taught, the technology being used, and the understanding of unique student needs. In merging these various instructional elements, the instructor must be comfortable as both a facilitator and content provider.

Faculty must develop skills that are beneficial in a traditional classroom setting, but essential if distant teaching is to be effective. Bronstein, Gill, and Koneman (1982) and Boone (1984) summarize these skills as follows:

* Be prompt in coming on line and insist that students do the same.
* Speak slowly, clearly, and use a natural style of delivery.
* Maintain a spontaneous delivery style and avoid reading, as if from a script.
* Consistently use effective visuals.
* Make frequent changes in pace to maintain interest.
* Frequently draw participants into discussions.
* Consistently refer to individual participants by name.
* Briefly summarize the concepts that are presented in each class session.
* Use authority consistently.
* Control verbal traffic.
* Provide social and emotional support by integrating late participants and encouraging humor.

- Create a democratic atmosphere in which authority is shared.
- Create a feeling of shared space and history.
- Exhibit appropriate behavior as a model for others.
- Seek and clarify common terms.
- Establish and maintain an appropriate pace.

Developing these skills takes time and significant energy, not only in planning and teaching the course, but also in self-critiquing the course's instructional effectiveness and revising the methods and means as appropriate. The result will prove rewarding to both instructor and students. As mentioned earlier, many instructors feel that the planning, preparation, and consideration required in distance education improves their face-to-face teaching as well.

3.4 Facilitators

In many distance-delivered courses, the instructor finds it beneficial to use a site facilitator to help in the effective delivery of course content, to enhance the use of instructional materials, and to ensure that course goals and objectives are met. The facilitator acts as a bridge between the students and instructor, keeping informed of student interests and progress, and providing guidance and answering questions as needed.

To be effective, a facilitator must understand the students being served and the expectations of the course instructor. Most importantly, the facilitator must be willing to follow the directives established by the teacher.

Where budget and logistics permit, the role of the on-site facilitator has increased in importance. Instructors who are unable to meet with students on a regular basis rely on facilitators to extend the impact of the instructor by meeting one-on-one with students. At the very least, they act as the instructor's on-site eyes and ears.

Teachers and facilitators need to agree on respective roles before the start of class. Typically, the role of the facilitator falls into one of three possible categories.

3.4.1 On-site facilitators with specific content expertise. Facilitators help explain difficult concepts and relate them to the students enrolled in the course. They are especially valuable in courses requiring laboratory experiences. In this case, the facilitator acts as a lab assistant in providing advice, distributing necessary materials, demonstrating proper procedure, and ensuring safety.

Facilitators with content knowledge may be in greater abundance than the instructor initially suspects. Most communities will have teachers or individuals in the general population with the requisite background and skills to fill this important role.

3.4.2 Facilitators with limited content expertise. While strong content knowledge is valuable, it's not essential. A facilitator with only limited content background still adds a personal dimension to a course otherwise unavailable when the actual instructor is miles away.

A well-utilized facilitator picks up student cues regarding interest, motivation, and performance that are unavailable to the distant teacher. In addition, the facilitator can provide extra attention to course participants who require or request it.

3.4.3 Facilitators with no content expertise. Most instructors find it reassuring to know there is someone on site to set up and troubleshoot equipment, distribute course materials, collect assignments, and proctor tests. Similarly, students find it helpful to have a person available locally if they have special needs, a class-related emergency, or must get a message to the instructor.

When available, the facilitator should be considered an important part of the team and a full participant in the teaching and learning process.

3.5 Support Staff

Support staff are the silent heroes of successful distance education programs. As with most educational endeavors, it is critical to understand and resolve the myriad details of program delivery that spell success or failure. Successful distance education programs typically centralize support service functions.

These consolidated functions include duplicating and distributing material (course syllabus, tests, handouts, etc.); ordering and distributing textbooks; sending and receiving grading reports; admissions and records; providing media and production services; scheduling and troubleshooting technical resources; resolving credit transfer issues; scheduling rooms, etc.

In short, the support service function is the glue that keeps the distance education enterprise together. Both students and faculty will find it invaluable to have a single organization coordinating the numerous support activities required for effective distance learning.

3.6 Administration

Administrators are typically influential in setting a direction for an institution's distance education program, but often lose contact once the program is running. This is unfortunate, because experience has shown that administrative leadership and continuing interest and support are essential to the long-term nurturing and growth of distance education programs.

Part of the problem lies in the fact that some administrators have limited teaching experience and even less background in the technical dimensions of the distance-delivery system. Often they relinquish their authority and decision-making to technical managers. Too often, this leads to growth in the technical infrastructure but a weakening of the academic underpinnings that are critical to the long-term success of distance education.

Effective distance education administrators are more than idea people. They are consensus builders, decision-makers, and facilitators. They maintain control of technical managers, ensuring that technological resources are effectively deployed to further the institution's academic mission. At the same time, they lead and inspire faculty and staff in overcoming obstacles that arise.

Most importantly, they maintain an academic focus, realizing that meeting the instructional needs of distant students is their ultimate responsibility.

3.7 In Summary

Effective distance education requires the integrated interest, participation, and enthusiasm of faculty, students, facilitators, support staff, and administrators. The informed involvement of these related participants won't avoid all problems, but it will help to meet the challenges that are sure to arise.

4.0

Faculty Development: Making the Most of In-Service Training

4.1 What Is Faculty Development and Why Is It Important in Distance Education?

Effectively teaching at a distance (and enjoying it) requires specialized skills, abilities, and training. While some teachers have instinctively developed the requisite skills and abilities, the majority require specialized training or trial and error to become comfortable and effective at a distance. Adequate training prior to distant teaching and continuing support throughout the delivery process are the most effective and efficient methods for ensuring long-term instructional success in distance education.

Although the term faculty development appears in various contexts, its definition is generally concerned with enhancing the talents, expanding the interests, improving the competence, and facilitating the professional and personal growth of faculty members, primarily in their role as instructors (Gaff, 1975).

The field of faculty development has evolved significantly since its inception. Past approaches focused on the symptoms of the problem (i.e., disenchanted students, falling enrollments, etc.) as

37

opposed to the problem itself: the lack of teacher effectiveness training. As a result, early efforts in the field of faculty development were concerned with curriculum change, recruiting brighter students as well as new doctoral faculty, reducing the student/faculty ratio, and developing instructional resource centers.

Faculty development strategies in recent years have taken a different approach by focusing on the improvement of instructional quality. Other practices attempt to help the faculty members to better understand themselves as teachers and individuals as well as the institution in which they work (Centra, 1976).

If the need for, and inherent challenges of, faculty development is important in traditional classroom settings, it is truly imperative in non-traditional settings in which distance delivery methods are employed. The need for faculty development in distance education has received national attention by teachers and administrators (see Gilcher & Johnstone, 1988), although relatively little has been written about it (see Moore & Thompson, 1990).

While few dispute that course content remains fundamentally unchanged regardless of the delivery method, those with distant teaching experience would likely echo the claim that thoughtful course adaptation is required if the distance-delivered instruction is to be effective.

If the distance education enterprise is systemwide and intended to meet the needs of rural and urban learners from widely different educational, cultural, social, and economic backgrounds, the challenges faced by the instructor increase exponentially. Without an understanding of the targeted learners and an ability to look at the content through their eyes, instructors are at a distinct disadvantage and may be discouraged from teaching future distance-delivered courses.

Another perplexing faculty development challenge relates to the technical and administrative infrastructure in place at many institutions. Historically and on a national level, technical managers have played a more dominant role than educators in distance education planning and implementation. Although much time is spent convincing funding agencies, governing boards, politicians, and fellow administrators that distance education technology is the solution, faculty are seldom consulted as to the nature of the problem. Given the fact that a poorly defined problem has an infinite number of solutions, faculty members are often expected to make a system function that they had little input in planning and that may or may not be instructionally appropriate.

Often, administrators and technical managers realize this conundrum after the technological system is in place. The academic reality dawns slowly that the interest, support, and enthusiasm of the faculty is required if a distance education program is to be successful, regardless of its technological sophistication. Enter faculty development and the need to plan and implement effective in-service training programs.

4.2 How Can Factors Inhibiting Faculty Development Be Overcome?

Typically, in-service training and faculty support programs rely on workshops, seminars, support groups, and hands-on training, in tandem with print and non-print instructional materials.

The goal of faculty development is change. This change must occur not only in the way instruction is delivered, but in the way the instructor sees the learner. Change in a complex educational environment is often difficult to accept, let alone promote. Kurpius and Christie (1978) identified and described four characteristics of the educational environment that inhibit change and must be overcome if faculty development efforts are to be effective. These factors are low interdependence among staff, high vulnerability, goal ambiguity, and individual orientation. After describing each factor, strategies for addressing them are discussed.

4.2.1 Low Interdependence Among Staff. The rigid departmental structure in many academic institutions affords few opportunities for instructors to receive advice, trade ideas, or collaboratively solve problems. This isolation leads to faculty insecurity regarding their own effectiveness in the classroom and tends to protect those lacking the motivation and desire to improve teaching skills.

To overcome this reality, the establishment of mentoring programs should be considered to bring new and veteran distance education faculty together in a non-threatening environment to share ideas and join together in joint problem solving.

4.2.2 High Vulnerability. Educational institutions, and the faculty who staff them, are subject to criticism as well as various demands from the immediate societal environment. As a result, faculty are often leery of programs that appear open to criticism.

Too often, the delivery of instruction at a distance is considered a new approach to education, and as a result is especially vulnerable to criticism. In reality, the novelty of distance education is more perception than reality. In one form or another and under various labels (e.g., correspondence study, independent learning) distance education has been an accepted educational approach for decades.

Studies have shown that the delivery method *per se*, whether face-to-face or technology assisted, has little to do with student performance. What matters is that delivery methods be appropriate to the content delivered and the characteristics of the learners. To overcome faculty perceptions of vulnerability, distance delivery methods must be

- appropriate to the requirements of the content,
- appropriate in their incorporation of relevant content examples,
- transparent to the learner, and
- appropriate and easy to use by faculty and students.

Once these conditions are met, faculty development experiences, including hands-on training, can reduce the vulnerability that faculty feel as they initially get involved with distant teaching.

4.2.3 Goal Ambiguity. As a result of various expectations, educational systems often work toward a number of contrasting and poorly defined goals. In addition, pressure to clarify intended outcomes can lead to the development of noncritical but easily measured goals.

To reduce goal ambiguity, institutions and departments participating in distance education should ensure that these teaching efforts are related to institutional and departmental missions, goals, and objectives. If, for example, a program goal is to meet the needs of underserved students, the characteristics and needs of those underserved students should be described, and more importantly, understood in detail by the faculty and administration.

4.2.4 Individual Orientation. Neither collaborative nor systematic, the individual orientation approach to education is dependent on solving educational problems by changing students, staff, and faculty within the system. Applied to student problems, for example, the individual orientation suggests that the institution is organized to meet the needs of all students. As a result, emphasis is placed on modifying the individual to meet the demands of the system, rather than changing the system to serve learners' needs.

Effective distance education requires that the individual needs and characteristics of both the students and faculty are considered when selecting delivery methods. The extent to which this is accomplished will have much to do with the effectiveness of the faculty development process and the distance teaching that results.

4.3 What Characteristics Make In-Service Training Effective?

Effective in-service faculty training programs take many forms. At some institutions, one-on-one sessions are used, while others rely on self-paced materials or campus-wide faculty development workshops. In terms of content expertise, some schools use external consultants and content experts, while others rely on internal resources for the development, adaptation, and implementation of distance education. Still others blend outside expertise with internal support to create an atmosphere of mutual support and group problem solving.

Regardless of the format or institutional approach to faculty development, successful in-service training experiences should share the following characteristics:

• Faculty participants should be encouraged to share concerns and question the administrative expectations of the technical system. Of equal importance is the honesty with which their concerns are addressed. Administrators should avoid excuses for not involving faculty earlier in the planning process. They should frankly discuss how the distance delivery system evolved and what its role will be, as envisioned by planners. Ideally, a formalized needs assessment will have been conducted and will serve as a combination rationale for change and blueprint for action.

• Technical systems should be described in the language of the user, not the technician, and incorporate easily understood and jargon-free language and related visuals. "Techno-babble" has no place in effective faculty development programs. It is the job of technical staff to speak in terms that are easily understood by educators. It is not the job of educators to become versed in the technical language of system managers.

• The goal of providing assistance in adapting traditional instruction for a non-traditional environment, not making "bad" instruction "good," should be established early and emphasized throughout in-service training.

• The importance of faculty ownership of the distance-delivered instruction should be emphasized. The faculty developer's job is to provide options and related rationale without wresting project control and decision-making from the instructor.

- If a distance education training workshop is planned, it should be a hands-on experience, with faculty getting first-hand experience using the technologies with which they'll be teaching. Technical assistance should be available, with advice offered in a supportive and jargon-free manner. The role of technical staff should be advisory and not set the tone or direction of in-service training activities. This same advisory role should be maintained during the implementation of distance delivery programs.

- Workshops should give faculty an opportunity to experience the "behind the scenes" work of technical staff. Also, faculty should sample the distance learning experience from the student's perspective.

- The opportunities, challenges, and difficulties faculty face in distance education settings should be discussed, using a realistic appraisal of the system's strengths and weaknesses.

- Practical strategies that can be immediately applied should be offered. These include managing distance education, tracking student participation, evaluating instructional effectiveness, and understanding the needs of distant learners.

- Through contact with potential students and interaction with other faculty, distance delivery instructors should be assisted in developing an understanding of and sensitivity to the social, cultural, educational, and economic backgrounds of the intended students. This understanding and appreciation will make for a more effective instructor and a more appreciative group of learners.

- Examples are the primary means by which content is presented. Faculty may require assistance in finding or developing content-related examples that are relevant to the distant learner.

- Alternative roles that faculty, students, and support staff play in a distance education context should be explored. Many successful distance educators have found, for example, that their role expands beyond that of content provider. They become skilled facilitators as well, drawing students out and encouraging full participation.
- Patterns of communication going beyond the more traditional teacher-student and student-content interaction should be discussed. The role of student-student interaction should be explored, including techniques for enhancing it.
- Faculty networks of those involved in distance education should be developed and nurtured on local, regional, national, and international levels. The on-going linkages they kindle and their potential for collective problem solving is invaluable.
- The majority of faculty development time and resources should be focused on interested, enthusiastic, and committed faculty. Some faculty won't be interested in teaching at a distance. Rather than spend time and resources attempting to convince the intractable, focus on those who want to learn effective distance delivery techniques, or at least have an open mind to the opportunities such techniques offer. In addition, supporting the early adopters often leads to the interest and eventual participation of the initially skeptical.
- Develop and nurture mentoring programs matching experienced distance education faculty with newcomers. While useful, shared content expertise in these mentoring experiences is not essential.
- The relationship of distance education and the institutional reward structure, such as promotion, tenure, and publishing, must be dealt with by

administrators in a proactive manner. It should be realized that in order to be effective, distance education must be viewed as a critically and academically sound mode of teaching, prominently reflected in the institutional reward structure.

4.4 Why Pay Special Attention to Promotion, Tenure, and the Academic Legitimacy of Distance Education?

Educational institutions expect teachers of distance-delivered courses to take their responsibilities seriously, devoting the time and effort needed to be successful. In return, it is appropriate that educational institutions recognize the legitimacy of distance teaching and reward this effort as they would more traditional forms of instructional delivery.

While strides have been made in recent years, some institutions and academic departments inaccurately view distance education as a second-class delivery method, not on par with traditional face-to-face instruction.

As previously stated, the distant teacher must not only know the content but also develop an understanding of distant student needs. Further, the instructor must become familiar with the technological delivery system and help students do the same, while simultaneously ensuring that the same levels of student performance required in traditional classes are maintained.

Because distant students are typically not integrated into day-to-day campus life and may have limited contact with other departmental faculty, they may not be as vocal in singing the praises of an exceptional instructor. Also, distant teaching often takes place behind closed doors, at times when traditional classes are not in session.

As a result, the work of the distant instructor may be forgotten or discounted during promotion and tenure proceedings. Effective administrators will be aware of these potential pitfalls and ensure that distant faculty are fairly evaluated and rewarded for their distance teaching efforts.

4.5 In Summary

While there are many pathways leading to successful faculty development in a distance education context, all have in common an informed understanding of specific program needs and goals. Successful faculty development programs evolve through a process that is methodical, flexible, and thoughtful.

The challenge is to match faculty development content and experiences to the needs of the instructors, and ultimately, the needs of students. The extent to which this is accomplished will dictate the success or failure of the faculty development effort.

5.0
Developing and Adapting Distance-Delivered Instruction

5.1 Why Formalize the Instructional Development Process?

As the term implies, instructional development is a systematic process for developing instruction. The process of instructional development provides a road map to the creation or adaptation of instruction, regardless of the delivery methods used.

Instructional development, as a formalized process, began in the early 1970s and resulted from the growing realization that the majority of university educators were schooled in professional disciplines (e.g., engineering, business, medicine, etc.), with little formal teacher training. Up to this point, many believed that effective teaching was an intuitive process as opposed to a learned skill. Either you were a good teacher or you weren't. It was further believed that the teacher's responsibility was to provide information, and the student's responsibility was to learn it.

Research in the field of educational psychology indicated, however, that the process of learning was significantly more complex, requiring systematic design and development to be effective. This well planned and highly organized approach to the creation of instruction increased as new technological delivery tools became available. Instructional technologists found that systematically developing instruction prior to media production was more cost- and time-effective than creating an expensive educational program only to find it to be instructionally ineffective.

Today, few would question that both teaching and learning are complex tasks. This is all the more true when the teacher and students have little in common. For this reason, many distance educators find it useful to follow the procedural guide provided by instructional development.

5.2 What Is Different About Distance Delivery?

As previously stated, in a traditional face-to-face classroom setting, the effective teacher constantly adapts course content and the resulting instruction based on a variety of visual cues provided by the students. By being co-located with students, the teacher is able to talk with them after class, observe them out of class, and get a better feel for students as individuals.

When teaching at a distance, however, many of these cues are absent. Faced with this dearth of information and the resulting discomfort, some teachers avoid the issue altogether by teaching the course as they had in the past without taking these new elements into consideration. Rather than solve the problem, this typically exacerbates it and creates an atmosphere of frustration for both teacher and students.

5.3 The Process of Instructional Development

The process of instructional development provides a non-threatening and systematic way to re-analyze and revise course content based on the unique characteristics and needs of the students. This is essential if distance-delivered instruction is to be effective.

The key to effective instructional development is finding the appropriate balance between the process itself and the resulting instruction. While different instructional development models abound, the vast majority follow the same basic developmental map (see Figure 1). This map consists of four basic landmarks: design, development, evaluation, and revision.

The process of instructional development is systematic and cyclical in that each stage leads to the next, with the final stage (i.e., revision) leading to reanalysis of the instruction, beginning with design.

5.4 The Design Stage

The design stage of the instructional development process begins with the identification and definition of an instructional problem or need. In planning to develop or adapt a course, the assumption is made that there is an instructional gap between what is and what should be. The instruction that results should fill this gap.

5.4.1 Understanding the Problem or Need. To further understand the dimensions of this gap, a number of questions should be asked, including:

Figure 1: The Instructional Development Process

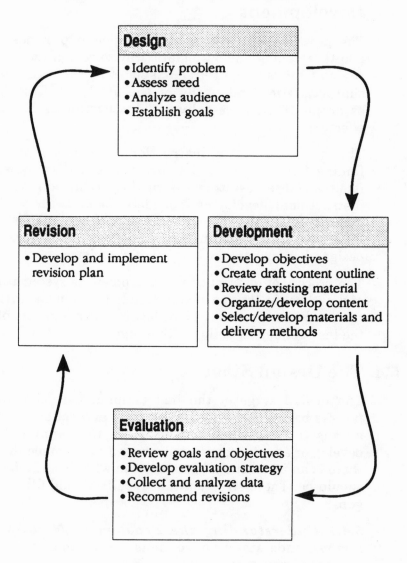

(Art by Paula Elmes)

- Why is the instruction needed?
- What are the specific needs of the target audience?
- What external data verify the need?
- What factors led to the instructional need?
- What past experiences indicate that the instruction being planned can effectively meet this need?

5.4.2 Understanding the Audience. To be effective, a detailed understanding of the target audience is required. To develop this understanding, ask a number of questions, including:

- What are the ages, cultural backgrounds, interests, and educational levels of the students?
- How familiar are the students with the various instructional methods and technological delivery systems under consideration?
- How will the audience apply the knowledge gained in the course, and how is it sequenced with other courses?
- Is the class composed of multicultural students or can they be categorized into several broad subgroups (e.g., rural-urban, graduate-undergraduate), each with different characteristics?

Answering these questions isn't easy, especially when teacher and students have little in common. Under these circumstances, the teacher should contact other instructors experienced in teaching the targeted student population.

Another technique is to contact and get to know students individually. Asking a few well-chosen questions will help to develop an understanding of their needs, backgrounds, and expectations. In addition, students will realize they are cared about as individuals.

5.4.3 Identifying Instructional Goals. In the design stage of the instructional development process, we are concerned with identifying very broad goals, based on content requirements and audience needs.

While goals are broad statements of instructional intent, objectives are quite specific. More importantly, they build together and lead to goal attainment.

5.4.4 Design in Summary.

1. *Identify your instructional problem or need:*
   - Why is the instruction needed?
   - What factors led to identification of this need?
   - How can the breadth and depth of the need be validated?
   - What are the differing views as to content to be included?
2. *Analyze the audience:*
   - How large is the audience?
   - What are their ages and cultural, social, and economic backgrounds?
   - What are their course-related levels of interest?
   - What experience do they have in distance learning?
3. *Develop instructional goals:*
   - Based on the instructional problem.
   - Focused on the needs of the target audience.

5.5 The Development Stage

In the design stage, the focus was on planning and gathering pertinent background information. In the development stage, that plan is put into action.

5.5.1 From Goals to Objectives. Based on an understanding of student characteristics and needs, in tandem with content requirements and course goals, individual objectives are developed that build together in meeting course goals. To use a building analogy, instructional goals are the walls of the course. The objectives are the individual bricks that join together in forming the walls.

This step-by-step approach to developing objectives will help ensure that the topic is systematically examined and that major issues are covered in a logical and sequential order.

Objectives should be

- stated in precise terms describing what should be done;
- written as descriptions of performance and stated in measurable terms;
- worded clearly so that learning experiences can be developed to meet each objective; and
- built together in hierarchical order.

In recent years, educators have vigorously debated the pros and cons of using measurable performance objectives. Opponents suggest that performance objectives unduly channel all learners down a single, inflexible, instructional path. Proponents maintain that precise performance objectives make both teachers and students more accountable.

Although this debate continues, it is clear that many teachers find instructional objectives to be invaluable in the development and adaptation of distance-delivered courses. They eliminate performance-related guesswork for both teacher and students.

5.5.2 Create a Content Outline. After developing objectives, create a rough outline of the content to be covered based on the audience analysis, instructional goals, objectives, and an understanding of the course content.

5.5.3 Review Existing Materials and Available Expertise. Locate and review currently available content-related print and non-print materials. It is often more cost- and time-efficient to use or adapt existing material than to develop it from scratch. However, avoid the use of materials or media just because they are available.

Also at this stage, seek the input and guidance of others with content expertise for purposes of review and critique. The course instructor is the focal point, bringing elements of the course together. This doesn't mean, however, that the teacher must go it alone. By having others with content expertise review course components, the end product will be both stronger and instructionally more effective.

5.5.4 Organize and Develop Content to Meet Objectives. Reorganize, revise, and refine the content outline to correspond to the order and content needs indicated by the objectives. Then, develop the content required to meet the objectives.

One of the greatest challenges facing someone developing or adapting a course for distance delivery is creating student-relevant examples. This is because content, for the most part, is taught through the use of examples relating the content being taught to a context understood by the students. The best examples form a bridge connecting the new content to a context that is familiar to the students. If the content examples are relevant for instructor and students, both teaching and learning are enhanced.

Unfortunately, distant students often have difficulty grasping the content being presented because the content examples lack relevance. This is especially true in multi-cultural situations where the teacher's realm of experience is quite different from that of the students.

It is often difficult for teachers to grasp the idea that the content examples they grew comfortable with over time and proved effective in traditional classroom settings are inappropriate to distance learning. Still, if the instruction is to be effective, the instructor must look beyond personally relevant examples and focus on contextual examples that hold relevance for the learner.

5.5.5 Select and Develop Materials and Delivery Systems. Base the selection and development of materials and delivery methods on audience characteristics and needs, content-based goals and objectives, and the constraints being faced, such as time and funding.

No technical delivery system is perfect. The challenge is to capitalize on the system capabilities that are appropriate to the instructional task at hand. Most often this requires the integrated use of various media and technology, including voice, video, data, and print.

5.5.6 Development in Summary.
1. *Develop course objectives:*
   • Be precise in your wording and performance expectations.
   • Word objectives to reflect the learning experiences they will measure.

- Assemble objectives into a learning hierarchy.
2. *Create a content outline:*
   - Incorporate your understanding of the need or problem.
   - Take into account the characteristics of the target audience.
   - Include all content requirements.
   - Make sure it reflects course goals and objectives.
3. *Review existing materials:*
   - Adapt existing materials as appropriate.
4. *Seek additional expertise:*
   - Build in outside expertise and review.
5. *Organize content:*
   - Structure content based on your combined understanding of the content, the learners, and instructional needs to be addressed.
6. *Select delivery approaches:*
   - Understand constraints and limitations with which you are faced, such as time and funding.
   - Understand strengths and weaknesses of different delivery alternatives.
7. *Develop materials:*
   - Integrate various delivery systems, including voice, video, data, and print, as appropriate.
   - Base the materials development effort on student characteristics, content requirements, and intended outcomes.

5.6 The Evaluation Stage

At its most basic level, the purpose of educational evaluation is to provide information to decision-makers. In distance education, there are many different types of decisions to be made and individuals charged with making them. For example:

- Students deciding whether to take a distance-delivered course are interested in the effectiveness of the instructor, the relevance of the content, and the appropriateness of the course in meeting some longer-term goal.
- Academic administrators deciding whether to include distant courses in their program must consider the costs of such an undertaking, appropriateness of the available delivery systems, the equivalence of traditional and non-traditional teaching standards, and the goals of their academic department or college.
- Institution administrators use information for planning and to ensure that the institutional mission is being addressed.
- Faculty use evaluation to assess student attitudes regarding teaching style, teaching effectiveness, and content relevancy. This information is used to critique and improve the course as well as their individual teaching style.

All of these decision-makers have one thing in common. They require evaluative information that is objective, accurate, and, most of all, useful.

5.6.1 What Makes Evaluation Useful? A number of characteristics have been identified that can improve the usefulness of educational evaluation (Brookfield, 1990, pp.139–141). These elements include:

- *Immediacy*: Timely feedback greatly enhances the chances that it will be used by decision-makers. This requires a balance between rigorous data collection and analysis and getting results to the people who can use them.

- *Clarity*: Make recommendations as clear as possible. Summarize the intent, process, and results of the evaluation in clear and concise language. Avoid jargon and terminology unfamiliar to the intended audience.

- *Regularity*: If the evaluative effort will be ongoing, provide feedback in regularly scheduled increments. This will encourage consistent attention to the evaluation efforts and better ensure that the results of the evaluation will be used.

- *Accessibility*: Provide sufficient opportunities for dissemination and discussion of evaluative findings. It's not enough to have completed the evaluation. Results must be accessible to the audiences for which they are intended. This often requires multiple formats for the distribution of evaluation findings.

- *Individualized*: Understand the needs and motivations of decision-makers for whom the evaluation is intended. This will increase the chances that evaluative findings can and will be used.

- *Future-Oriented*: Provide clear suggestions regarding the specific actions that the target audience should make to implement the recommendations in the evaluation.

- *Justifiable*: All findings and recommendations should be firmly grounded in the data collection and analysis effort. Incorporate a system of checks and balances to identify and eliminate personal biases in the entire evaluation, from planning to implementation.

Improving the effectiveness of evaluation often requires different, yet complementary, levels of data collection and analysis. For example, when a distance-delivered course is being developed, the faculty member will likely require evaluative information as it is being developed (i.e., formative evaluation) as well as information regarding the overall effectiveness of the completed course (i.e., summative evaluation).

5.6.2 *Formative Evaluation.* Formative evaluation is considered "in process" evaluation because it is completed while the course is being developed and continues throughout the development and adaptation of a course for distance delivery. Its primary purpose is to ensure that the development effort remains on track and holds true to the instructional goals established in the planning stage of the instructional development effort. Formative evaluation is especially valuable with new audiences or when delivery systems are first used and the developer wants to ensure the accuracy of developmental assumptions.

Developing or adapting instruction for distance delivery is time consuming for the faculty member and costly in terms of the sophisticated delivery systems likely to be used. Those using formative evaluation operate under the assumption that it is better to develop a few representative units of instruction and related delivery components and field test them with the intended student audience than to develop the entire course only to find that it is fundamentally flawed.

Formative evaluation can be conducted on two or more levels. Level one typically includes a review of sample instructional materials by content experts. The intent is to ensure content accuracy and a comprehension level appropriate to the target audience.

A second level of formative evaluation would entail the actual delivery of one or more instructional components to the intended target audience. Using interviews, observations, objective tests, and attitudinal information, the developer would then determine the effectiveness of the instruction.

Formative evaluation allows improvement of the course as it is being developed or adapted. Most importantly, it is a good check to ensure that small instructional problems don't become insurmountable obstacles, remaining hidden until the course is completed and a significant investment in time and money has been made.

5.6.3 Summative Evaluation. Summative evaluation, as the name implies, is conducted upon completion of the course and seeks to determine the overall effectiveness of the finished instructional product. By this stage, general questions of content accuracy will have been answered. Now, the question becomes whether or not the students actually learned as a result of the course. This will require objective measures of student performance, which should compare favorably with traditionally taught versions of the course.

Additional summative feedback should focus on course relevancy (i.e., was the initial audience analysis accurate?) and learner attitudes towards the delivery approach and the instructor's teaching style.

Typically, faculty are most familiar and comfortable with developing and implementing objective measures of student performance through tests, quizzes, and assignments. For some faculty members, getting student feedback regarding the overall relevancy and effectiveness of a course can be threatening, since the evaluative focus changes from the student to the course itself and the teacher. For this reason, the summative evaluator should maintain sensitivity in balancing the intent of the evaluation with the full participation and enthusiasm of the faculty member. If the evaluator expects the results of the inquiry to be used for course improvement, the participating faculty must feel ownership of the evaluation.

5.6.4 Quantitative and Qualitative Evaluation Methods. The type of data collected in the formative and summative evaluation may be broadly categorized as either quantitative or qualitative. Quantitative evaluation relies on a breadth of response and is patterned after experimental research focusing on the collection and statistical manipulation of relatively large quantities of data. Evaluative conclusions emerge from the resulting statistical analysis.

In contrast, qualitative evaluation focuses on depth of response, highlighted by the gathering of detailed information and anecdotal data from a typically smaller group of respondents.

5.6.5 Quantitative Data Collection and Analysis. Although numerous quantitative evaluation methods exist, they are often categorical "forced choice" scales in which the student places himself in a certain category, or has his behavior categorized in a certain way. For example, Likert scales are popular survey instruments that often ask students to respond to statements in terms of their level of agreement. A typical Likert scale might use a 5-point scale with values ranging from "strongly agree" (numerical value 1) to "strongly disagree" (numerical value 5). Once tallied, these values are statistically analyzed and result in broad conclusions based on the level of agreement. For example, a statistically averaged value of 2 suggests that the respondents, in general, agree with the statement being made.

Quantitative evaluation is particularly useful when there will be large numbers of respondents for whom more in-depth, personalized approaches are not feasible. Its heavy reliance on statistical analysis improves its objectivity and diminishes the encroachment of the evaluator's subjective judgments. In addition, quantitative approaches are relatively quick and easy to administer and complete, making them less expensive to conduct than qualitative evaluations. They are especially useful when evaluating on-going programs that have been in existence for some time. The quantitative evaluation provides statistical information that may be of value to the researcher seeking to modify the instructional program, making minor adjustments as required.

Quantitative approaches can, however, pose significant drawbacks to the distance education evaluator:

- Many distance education courses have relatively small class sizes with students from various backgrounds for whom there is little baseline information. These small, stratified populations typically defy relevant statistical analysis.
- Quantitative surveys typically result in a rate of return of under 50 percent. A low rate of return often suggests that only those feeling very positively or negatively about the course responded to the evaluation. The silent majority lack the motivation to complete and return the evaluation instrument. Making programmatic adjustments based on a low return rate will typically lead to course revisions based on false assumptions.
- By definition and design, forced choice surveys offer respondents a limited number of possible response options. Therefore, fresh insights and unique

perspectives falling outside the provided response categories go unreported.

- The cumbersome and often tedious nature of quantitative data collection and analysis can discourage formative evaluation, and often results in an over-reliance on summative evaluation.
- Statistical analysis often results in an illusion of precision that may be far from reality. For example, if half of the respondents strongly agree with a statement (statistical value 1) and the other half strongly disagree with the same statement (statistical value 5), their averaged responses will be statistically neutralized (statistical value 3.0), masking the fact that students either strongly agree or disagree with the statement being made. This could encourage the instructional developer or faculty member to ignore the finding when the strong agreement or disagreement suggests a need for further investigation.

5.6.6 Qualitative Data Collection and Analysis. As the name implies, the focus here is on the quality of response and typically emphasizes the gathering of in-depth information from fewer respondents. The qualitative evaluator is concerned with observing behavior that might be open to differing subjective interpretations. As such, the qualitative evaluator must be aware of personal bias and collect data from multiple sources to ensure that observations are grounded in reality.

Guba (1978) identified a number of qualitative methods for collecting evaluative data, including:

- *Open-ended questioning* with respondents asked to identify course strengths and weaknesses, suggest changes, explore attitudes towards distance delivery methods, etc.

• *Participant observation* with the evaluator observing group dynamics and behavior while participating in the class as an observer, asking occasional questions, and seeking insights regarding the process of distance education.

• *Non-participant observation* with the evaluator observing a course (e.g., an audioconference, interactive television class, etc.) without actually participating or asking questions.

• *Content analysis* with the evaluator using predetermined criteria to review course documents including the syllabus and instructional materials submitted by the instructor as well as student assignments and course-related planning documents.

• *Interviews* with a facilitator or specially trained individual collecting evaluative data through one-on-one and small-group interviews with students.

• *Unobtrusive measures* are typically reserved for confirming or rejecting data collected through other means and may be used for observing, recording, and analyzing human behavior without the knowledge or awareness of those who are observed (Guba & Lincoln, 1981, p. 263). Unobtrusive measures would include the review of records such as class attendance lists and simple observations such as diagrams of classroom seating arrangements.

Central to the notion of qualitative evaluation is "triangulation," in which different types of data are collected and compared in efforts to confirm or reject evaluative hypotheses.

For example, the qualitative evaluator in a distance education setting might begin by sitting in as a non-participant observer during several class sessions. As a result, interview questions are formulated and administered, and followed up with the collection of class attendance and participation records. By comparing the results of the various data collection methods (triangulation), the evaluator discovers if all sources of information point to the same evaluative conclusions. If conclusions derived from different data collection methods conflict, the evaluator continues collecting data until clear and consistent conclusions can be drawn.

When collecting qualitative information for the first time, consider the following six focusing questions for gathering some baseline data. They will provide an insightful overview of student attitudes about the distance-delivered course and can be used as a foundation for more in-depth evaluative approaches.

1. List and describe five weaknesses of this course.
2. List and describe three strengths of this course.
3. If you were teaching this course, what would you do differently?
4. Would you recommend this course to a friend? Why or why not?
5. What should have been covered in this course but wasn't?
6. What additional comments or ideas can you offer at this time?

5.6.7 Evaluation in Summary. Whether the intent is formative or summative evaluation and whether data collection methods are quantitative or qualitative, obtaining accurate and useful evaluative information can best be done in a supportive and non-threatening environment. Remember to:

- Emphasize to students that the evaluation data will not be considered in assigning grades.
- If completing formative evaluation, let students know why you are collecting the information and how it will be used.
- If completing summative evaluation, let students know where, when, and how they may review the results of the evaluative effort.
- Don't administer the summative evaluation before a major test or when an assignment is due.
- Provide anonymity to those completing the evaluation.
- Consider having a non-instructional staff person administer and collect the completed evaluation.
- Leave adequate room for detailed responses, without intimidating respondents with large blocks of blank space.
- Provide class time for completing the evaluation.
- Keep evaluation questions brief and focused.
- As appropriate, consider combining quantitative and qualitative evaluation techniques.

5.7 The Revision Stage

There will be room for improvement in even the most carefully developed distance-delivered course. When dealing with anything as elusive as knowledge, understanding, and the subtle differences in learners, revisions should be expected. In fact, the instructor will likely have more confidence in a course that requires significant revision than in one that was supposedly flawless the first time through. If little is found requiring change, chances are course revision opportunities are being missed.

5.7.1 Planning for Revision. Most revision plans are a direct outcome of the summative evaluation. It should point out course strengths and weaknesses, as well as suggest specific areas needing revision. Another source of revision ideas will be feedback from colleagues and content specialists.

Possibly the best source of revision ideas will be the instructor's own reflections on course strengths and weaknesses. For this reason, it's a good idea to consider revision ideas within a week or two after the semester ends. Those who procrastinate in review and revision seldom improve the course before it is taught again.

Quite often, course revisions will be minor, such as breaking a particularly large and unwieldy instructional unit into more manageable components, increasing assignment feedback, or improving student-to-student interaction. At the same time, it is important to remember that the characteristics and needs of each distance-delivered class will vary, and that revisions required for one learner group may be inappropriate for a different student population.

On other occasions, needed revisions will be significant. If this occurs, revisions should be prioritized, focusing attention on the most important ones first. If revisions result in significant course changes, consider field-testing prior to future scheduling of the course.

5.7.2 Revision in Summary

- Allocate time for course revision before the end of class to ensure there is time to complete it.
- Use summative evaluation data, outside content review, and personal observations in the revision plan.

- If revisions are major, prioritize a schedule for completing them.
- Consider field testing significantly revised course components prior to teaching them again.
- Remember that even the best designed or adapted distance-delivered course will likely require revision.

5.8 Shortening the Instructional Development Process

As a final note, strict adherence to the systematic process of instructional development can help ensure a successful distance delivery experience for both teacher and students. By design, the process of instructional development is rigorous and demands focused attention. Still, the instructional development process should be viewed as a means to an end, not an end in itself. What if you have neither the time nor desire to complete the entire process? Can the process be shortened? The answer is yes.

Shortening the instructional development process, when time or energy is limited, is both possible and acceptable if it's done logically by focusing effort on the most critical elements of the course development or adaptation effort. When developing or adapting a distant course for first-time delivery to a new audience, the design and evaluation stages are typically the weak links demanding the most time and effort.

When traditional courses are developed or adapted for first-time delivery at a distance, the faculty member is typically most confident in the content being presented and least comfortable with the needs and character-istics of the distant student population. Without a con-certed effort to understand the instructional needs and unique characteristics of the distant learners, the course will lack the personal focus needed for it to be effective.

Adequate needs assessment, in tandem with formative and summative evaluation strategies, are critical foundational elements in all distance learning endeavors. Adequate time and energy spent here will help ensure the effectiveness of the newly developed or adapted course and facilitate the successful completion of any future revisions that might be required.

5.9 In Summary

Instructional Development for Distance Delivery:

Design Stage:
- Identify the instructional problem.
- Assess instructional needs.
- Analyze the audience.
- Develop instructional goals.

Development Stage:
- Develop course objectives.
- Create a content outline.
- Review existing materials.
- Seek additional expertise.
- Organize content.
- Select delivery methods and technology.
- Develop materials.

Evaluation Stage:
- Select appropriate quantitative and qualitative data collection measures.
- Plan and implement formative evaluation.
- Plan and implement summative evaluation.

Revision Stage:
- Allow adequate time for revision.
- Use summative evaluation data.
- Use personal observations.
- Use outside peer feedback.
- Prioritize items to be revised.
- Complete revisions as prioritized.

6.0
Selecting Appropriate Teaching Tools and Technology

6.1 Selecting Tools for the Task

Vast assortments of technological options are available to the distance educator. These options include interactive audioconferencing, one- and two-way video, computer conferencing, audio graphic systems, as well as print (see Educational Technology Publications, 1991).

While most distance educators consider themselves educators first and technologists second, many get distracted by new technological developments. When it comes to "distance education," some tend to focus too much attetion on overcoming "distance" through the use of technology, and not enough attention on the resulting "education."

Making premature technological decisions without adequate planning is damaging for several reasons:

- Basing technological decisions on emotion, impatience, ignorance, politics, or whim typically results in failure. These failures tend to limit the future effectiveness of faculty and administrators tied to the earlier, poorly planned efforts.

• Institutions considering the development of distance education capabilities often fail to keep faculty informed as technological plans develop. When the system is put in place, they wonder why faculty don't immediately accept and support the new delivery system.

• Even limited field testing of distance education technology requires a large capital investment for multi-site linkages. Each site will require complementary, if not identical, equipment. In addition, this equipment base will often require a combination of voice, video, and data technology.

• Often, distance education requires a technological infrastructure to make use of the equipment actually placed on site. For example, video transmission often requires an investment in microwave or satellite technology, while coordinated systemwide audioconferencing may require centralized bridges and sophisticated conference scheduling software.

The cost efficiencies of such wide-scale distribution systems are most evident when many sites are linked. Often, there is pressure on an institution, department, or individual administration to commit to a specific technological approach.

Committing to a technological approach as a result of institutional pressure is shortsighted and will likely lead to long-term problems.

• Many technologies are incompatible. To the uninitiated, similar capabilities would seem to suggest that various families of technology include interchangeable components. This is seldom the case. The result can be a great variety of equipment that is similar in capabilities, but technically incompatible.

Before purchasing technology, it is wise to conduct field tests where the proposed technology is integrated with other system components. Prior to making a purchasing decision, the prospective buyer should talk to other users who have incorporated a similar technological interface. Equipment vendors should not be relied on to explain the technological weaknesses of their systems.

- Once new equipment has been placed on site, it should be tested thoroughly to ensure it operates correctly. This should be done promptly, whether or not final installation is immediately planned.

  Many institutions fail to test system components until all components are on site. Unfortunately, by the time all parts of the system have arrived, individual warranties may have expired.

  To avoid this problem, vendors should either complete a systems check as components are received, or extend warranties until full-scale implementation has been completed.

- Engineering and technical support expertise often focuses on specific equipment types, even makes and models. As new technologies are integrated into existing systems; or upgrading takes place, the institution is often faced with adding technical staff to support these additional equipment purchases or retraining existing personnel.

  These concerns increase dramatically when outlying sites requiring technical support are factored in. It is wise to include all related personnel and support costs when considering the purchase of the new system. In fact, some form of life-cycle costing should be implemented to ensure that both short- and long-term maintenance funds are available.

- Like hardware, most system software is manufacturer specific, quite expensive, and not readily adaptable to rapidly evolving technical advancements.

The costs associated with software purchase and upgrade must be considered at the same time distance education hardware purchases are contemplated.

- Factor related costs (instructional and software development) into overall system budgets.

Many institutions fund only hardware, assuming that granting agencies will bridge the financial gap with supplemental support for software and personnel. Often they don't. A more responsible approach is to simultaneously fund hardware acquisition and software development, including support costs.

- Distance education technology is rapidly changing. If planning does not precede initial equipment commitments, the users may be strapping themselves to a system that meets short-term requirements without the requisite core capabilities needed for future expansion. This could lead to abandoning the initial technological innovation when longer-term needs are considered.

Although the ability to expand from a solid technological foundation is a worthy instructional goal, rapidly developing voice, video, and data technology makes this difficult and encourages every distance educator to be a futurist, capable of looking beyond short-term needs.

Involving key user groups in the planning process can help avoid costly technological mistakes. Most technical pitfalls associated with distance education are avoidable through adequate assessment of instructional needs. While adequate planning takes time, consideration, and hard work, it is a small investment compared to the ramifications of forgoing this important step.

6.2 Technological Growth, Demise, and Revival

The tendency of some distance educators to make premature decisions about delivery systems often leads to technological growth, demise, and revival. The following illustrates how this cycle typically unfolds.

6.2.1 Growth Stage. In the growth stage, either an administrator, faculty member, or staff technologist develops a hunch that a particular technology will meet some obvious, but poorly defined, distance education need. Rather than develop an academically grounded understanding of the need to be met, the need is perceived to be so obvious that the decision is made to proceed with the selection and implementation of a technological delivery system.

Without adequate planning, however, legislative or institutional funding is difficult to obtain. To encourage funding, system capabilities are over-promoted, using unsubstantiated claims of cost effectiveness and efficiency, technical reliability, and instructional effectiveness. To keep projected costs low, budgets are submitted for hardware purchases alone, based on the false belief that software, maintenance, and personnel funding will follow. In addition, hopelessly optimistic timelines are developed.

The selected system is usually championed by an influential legislator or administrator. Once the equipment arrives, typically late, vendor support is found to be less than expected or needed. At about the same time, the institution's technical managers realize the system is more complex than anticipated, numerous equipment bugs are discovered, and third-party vendors can't deliver as promised.

By this point, overly optimistic timelines are outdated and the legislators and administrators who originally championed the system are demanding the results that were promised when funding was being sought. As the poorly conceived technological plan unravels, those associated with it run for cover.

6.2.2 Demise Stage. In the demise stage, it becomes more difficult for the technological promoters to hide the fact that expectations aren't being met and that long-promised system benefits are unrealistic.

At this point, technical promoters attempt to buy time by either blaming a third party for system difficulties or claiming that one or more pieces of auxiliary equipment are needed to make the system operational. Although financial managers may believe this initially, the realization dawns quickly that the technological solution was poorly planned and conceived, and that no reasonable amount of money is likely to rectify the problems.

Late in the demise stage, funding is withdrawn, either slowly or quickly, personnel are laid off, and the technological cure-all is put in storage.

6.2.3 Revival Stage. The revival stage begins when individuals realize that although the system can't match the expectations of technical promoters, it might be effective in meeting a more narrowly defined instructional need.

At this point, identifiable and well-understood learner needs are matched with realistic technical capabilities. As the system proves effective in meeting better-defined instructional goals, limited funding is reinstated and the system is implemented in a more cost-effective and instructionally sound manner.

There is only one way to avoid this costly cycle of frustration: Focus on tangible learner needs, before selecting instructional technology. Don't make the assumption that a delivery system that works in one instructional situation will automatically work in another. The educator's challenge is to select an appropriate mix of technology by focusing on an instructionally effective combination of the various technological tools available.

It is mystifying but true that institutions often repeat this three-stage cycle every few years, with the arrival of each new technological breakthrough. As leadership changes, institutional memory fades, and the same mistakes are repeated. It's not a question of institutional maturity. Large research institutions are as prone to this trap as small colleges, universities, and school districts. Until a more direct relationship exists in education between academic planning and technological decision-making, the problem is unavoidable.

With these concerns and caveats in mind, the focus will now change to the voice, video, data, and print tools available to the distance educator.

6.3 Voice Tools

There are many instructional audio tools available, including the interactive technologies of telephone, audioconferencing, and short-wave radio. Passive (i.e., one-way) audio tools include audio tapes and radio. Instructionally, these tools are used much like print. Instead of reading the content, however, the student listens to it. While the absence of interaction is sometimes problematic, both audio tapes and one-way radio can supplement more interactive forms of audio communication.

6.3.1 Interactive Audioconferencing. Since the early 1980s, audioconferencing has been a critical component of many distance education programs throughout the United States.

The University of Alaska, for example, maintains a central network with the capacity to link over 160 different sites in up to 30 simultaneous audio-conferences. This statewide system includes over 330 audioconference-equipped sites. The equipment consists of speakers and push-to-talk or voice-activated microphones. Using this system has proven to be more cost-effective than using many separate phone lines. In addition, audioconferencing equipment eliminates the need for users to hold a phone to their ear for extended periods of time and provides better sound quality. If equipment is not available, however, any ordinary telephone can be used.

Sponder (1990, 1991) offers an insightful look at the practice of instructional audioconferencing in rural Alaska. Because audioconferencing is convenient, effective, and easy to use, it has become a cornerstone in the delivery of educational services to students throughout Alaska.

6.3.2 Audioconferencing Advantages.

* It is an interactive medium, allowing direct student and instructor participation. Students have many opportunities for give and take with other students, the instructor, and outside experts.
* It provides many opportunities for direct feedback. Distant learners can participate in the planning

and developing of curriculum relevant to their needs.

- It fosters the development of learning experiences that are tailored to the needs of specific learners.
- It can be used to share information with participants from diverse areas.
- It facilitates discussion and feedback, allowing increased participation by students while decreasing the sense of isolation they may feel.
- It is cost-effective for rural or geographically dispersed learners.
- It can be very effective when used in combination with other media including print, video, and computers.

6.3.3 Audioconferencing Limitations.

- May encounter initial resistance until users become familiar with the equipment and how to use it effectively.
- Does not provide for graphic content. This can be difficult for the visually-oriented learner.
- Can be impersonal because it eliminates nonverbal cues, such as smiles, frowns, arm and hand movements, body language, etc.
- Is subject to technical difficulties that can interrupt the lesson and content flow.
- Places restrictions on the type of content that can be delivered in an oral format.
- Requires advance planning and preparation.
- Can encourage isolation if students are permitted to audioconference individually instead of in small groups.

- Is subject to toll charges that can be quite costly, depending on the number and location of participating sites.

6.3.4 Conducting an Audioconference Course. Generally, good teaching techniques are the same, whether the teacher and learner are in one room or separated by many miles. Still, some teaching techniques are more effective than others when using audioconferencing as an instructional medium.

It is important to remember that the major feature of audioconferencing is its two-way interactive capability. Understanding and using this feature is the key to conducting successful audioconference classes.

6.3.5 Conference Planning. As previously noted, effective planning is essential to successful distance education. In planning your instructional audio-conference:

- Determine learner characteristics.
- Establish realistic instructional goals and objectives.
- Incorporate content examples that are relevant to your learners.
- Plan short learning segments to avoid listener fatigue.
- Simplify the presentation to fit audio-only delivery.
- Don't present too much information over a short period of time.
- Encourage participation by building in segments for student feedback.
- Incorporate study questions to stimulate student participation and assignment completion.

- Arrange guest speakers well in advance and brief them on the role they will be playing.

6.3.6 Effective Audio Support Materials. To be effective, well-organized support materials are essential. Consider the following:

- Printed outlines to eliminate the need for excessive note-taking and for review purposes. They may be combined with topic outlines.
- Topic outlines that identify the major and minor concepts being covered, making it easy to refer to key points for lecture or questions. Leave free space for student notes.
- Written handouts with easy-to-reference headings. Use headings as reference points during lecture periods.
- Visual materials including slides, photos, and videotapes.
- Electronic communications such as text and graphics delivered via computer, electronic bulletin board, or audio graphics system.

6.3.7 Creating the Learning Environment.

- Create a relaxed atmosphere by beginning each conference with locally relevant questions requiring short answers.
- Emphasize that communication will become easier as students gain familiarity with technical equipment.
- Develop a sense of anticipation.
- Create group rapport through small-group work and other techniques to enhance student-to-student interaction.

6.3.8 Encouraging Participation.

- Plan for interactive periods using case studies, role-playing, and question-and-answer sessions.
- Assign study questions for future class discussion.
- Prepare the group for participation by emphasizing the importance of discussion and student-to-student interaction.
- Develop a roster with student names and locations. Use it to track student participation.
- Assign the responsibility of leading future class discussions to individual students or sites.
- Structure class participation using direct questions, student reports, interviews, and role playing.
- Control domination by any one individual or site.
- Listen attentively and acknowledge student contributions.

6.3.9 Humanizing the Audioconference.

Before the class meets:

- Send students a welcome letter, course syllabus, relevant course materials, available resources, contact people, and policies.
- Send students your photo and a short biographical sketch. If possible, have students exchange photos and biographical sketches.
- Conduct a pre-course audioconference to discuss the technology and processes of audioconferencing.

During the audioconference:

- Be yourself and speak in a conversational style.
- Vary your pacing.

- Begin class by taking roll and insist that students be punctual.
- Insist that all participants preface comments with their name and location.
- Allow adequate time for responses. Pause a minimum of 10 to 15 seconds before continuing or repeating your request for response.
- Respond directly to individual questions in a timely manner. Encourage students to telephone or write with questions and comments.
- Call on each student to ensure full participation.

After the audioconference:

- Request student input through discussion by telephone, computer, and mail.
- Make comments on written assignments. Be specific and encouraging.
- Encourage student meetings via audioconference, phone, computer, or mail.
- If possible, alternate the sites from which you teach. If that is not possible, try to meet with students if they pass through your town or vice versa.
- Try facilitating sessions in which students are responsible for leading discussions.

6.4 Video Tools

Instructional video tools include still images such as slides, pre-produced moving images (e.g., film, videotape), and real-time moving images combined with audioconferencing (one-way or two-way video with two-way audio).

Instructional television (ITV), is an especially popular distance education delivery system that can be integrated into the curriculum at three basic levels:

• *Single lesson.* Programs address one specific topic or concept, providing a lesson introduction, overview, or summary.

• *Selected unit.* A series of programs providing the content foundation for a learning unit in the course curriculum.

• *Full course.* Programs from one or more ITV series that provide an integrated, video-based course. Prepackaged telecourses, that are commercially produced and typically marketed with supplementary learning materials (text, teacher's guide, student guide), can also be effectively used.

Instructional television is broadly divided into passive and interactive categories. Passive instructional television, often sponsored by public television stations, is typically seen at home and might include such programs as National Geographic specials and NOVA. Other forms of passive ITV include single-concept instructional programs offering no opportunity for interaction either before, during, or after the program's conclusion.

In contrast, interactive ITV provides opportunities for viewer interaction, either with a live instructor or a student at a participating site. For example, two-way television with two-way audio allows all students to view and interact with the teacher (see Lochte, 1993). At the same time, cameras at remote sites allow the teacher to view all participating students. It is also possible to configure the system so that all student sites may view one another.

Using a one-way television with two-way audio format, students view the teacher via on-site television monitors, interacting with participants using audioconferencing equipment or speaker phones.

Another form of instructional television combines passive program viewing with occasional interactive sessions in which the instructor or facilitator meets with students to discuss instructional material.

Most distance educators would agree that the key to effective instruction is developing lesson plans promoting interactive viewing and involving the student in a variety of integrated learning activities.

6.4.1 Instructional Television Advantages.

- It is not intimidating. Most students grew up watching television.
- It provides motion and visuals together in a single format, which is an important component in many content areas. The old cliché, "a picture is worth a thousand words," rings true.
- Instructional television is a captivating tool. Visualization is inherently interesting.
- It can be used effectively as a motivational tool.
- It is particularly effective in introducing, summarizing, and reviewing concepts.
- It provides an effective way to visually take students to new environments (the moon, a foreign country, through the lens of a microscope, etc.).

6.4.2 Instructional Television Limitations.

- Broadcast quality ITV is often expensive to create and can cost well over $1,000 per finished minute to produce.

- Video production is time consuming and can be technically demanding, often requiring relatively sophisticated production facilities.
- Sites choosing to interactively participate in an ITV program may require specialized equipment, facilities, and staffing.
- Most prepackaged ITV courses use a mass media approach to instruction aimed at the average student. As a result, they can be ineffective in serving students with special needs.
- When used passively, without interactive capabilities, its instructional effectiveness can be limited.
- Unless professionally produced, completed ITV programs often look amateurish.
- Once completed, ITV programs are difficult to revise and update.

6.4.3 Conducting an Interactive ITV Lesson. Teaching a live class to students at remote sites using ITV and interactive audioconferencing can be instructionally effective, if the content and needs of the learners are appropriate. Still, it is important to remember that interactive ITV is not the same as face-to-face instruction in which teacher and students share the same physical space. Effective utilization requires systematic planning, organization, and the ability to remain flexibly focused on instructional goals. Towards this end, consider the following three-step plan:

1. *Set the Stage*
   - Prepare viewers for new terminology to be used in the program, and answer any questions regarding the technical equipment being used, such as cameras, television monitors, audio equipment, etc.

- Inform students if there will be camera operators or technicians in the classroom. Although the students may be initially curious, this will fade as the class progresses. In-class technicians are trained to be as unobtrusive as possible.

- When simultaneously instructing a live class and distant sites, make sure that questions and comments are addressed to all student participants.

- Organize all class materials and visuals before the start of class. It is best to have a trial run with technical staff so that all participants know the role they are expected to play.

- If you are electronically projecting visuals using an overhead camera, understand its operation and limitations prior to the start of class.

- Students should have the necessary background materials to make the best use of televised lessons. Consider the use of study questions to assist in focusing discussions.

- Practice in front of a live camera prior to class. If possible, have a colleague, a few target students, or a media technician view your presentation and on-camera presence, offering suggestions for improvement.

- If using outside speakers, give students necessary background information prior to class. Do the same with outside speakers. Let them know the specific purpose of their session, what is expected of them, and the general background of participating students.

- Remember that it takes longer to deliver instruction at a distance than in a traditional face-to-face setting. Plan lessons accordingly.

- Lead discussions to help students form generalizations and conclusions and to generate subject-related interest.

2. *During the Interactive Session*
   - Remain as attentive and involved in the televised lesson as you expect your students to be. Enthusiasm is contagious. So is boredom.
   - Motivate students and increase interest through the use of questions, examples, and case studies.
   - To help focus viewing, indicate key points to look for.
   - Review the concepts discussed in the program and clarify any misunderstandings by asking focused questions.
   - Integrate activities to reinforce the content presentation. These activities might include quizzes, worksheets, role-playing, and experiments. Teacher guides frequently provide creative ideas that can be adapted to the course.
   - Make sure opportunities are included to enhance student interaction throughout the session. Present content in five to ten minute blocks, interspersed with discussion.

3. *Following the Session*
   - Review taped recordings of the presentation, either with technical staff, a colleague, or by yourself. Take notes for improving your presentation, style, and delivery methods.
   - Seek student feedback on the strengths and weaknesses of the instructional materials and the teaching strategies being used.
   - Be open to new ideas and delivery techniques for improving instructional effectiveness.

6.5 Data Tools

Computers send and receive information electronically. It is for this reason that the term "data" is used to describe this broad category of instructional tools.

Computers have revolutionized all forms of instruction and come in all shapes and sizes. They may be the size of a typewriter (microcomputer), a small desk (minicomputer), or a large room (mainframe, super-computer).

As described by Verduin and Clark (1991), computer applications for distance education are varied. They include computer-assisted instruction (CAI), computer-managed instruction (CMI), computer-mediated education (CME), and computer-based multimedia (CBM).

6.5.1 Computer-Assisted Instruction (CAI). Computer-assisted instruction (CAI) uses the computer as a self-contained teaching machine to present individual lessons. These instructional units typically supplement more traditional classroom activities. There are several CAI modes, including: drill and practice, tutorial, simulations and games, and problem solving (see Heinich, Molenda, & Russell, 1985).

Tutorial and drill-and-practice modes rely on question-and-answer formats. Drill and practice exercises use repetition. Tutorials incorporate the basic interaction of a student and instructional tutor. Based on the response to a question or case study, the computer electronically moves (branches) the student to a segment of the instructional program. The branching nature of CAI programs provides different instructional sequences for different levels of student performance. For example, the student who initially responds correctly, is branched to progressively more advanced instructional content. The student responding incorrectly, in contrast, is cycled back for remedial instruction.

Educational simulations and games take real-world situations and reconstruct their essential elements, creating a system that reacts spontaneously to varied student responses. This form of learning requires the student to use inductive logic in developing rules or procedures for explaining the evidence provided in the data base.

Computer-based problem solving requires the student to define a problem before manipulating variables in efforts to solve it. The CAI program provides a data base of possible solutions to the problem under consideration.

6.5.2 Computer-Managed Instruction (CMI). Computer-managed instruction (CMI) uses the computer to organize instruction and track student records and progress. The instruction itself need not be delivered via a computer, although often CAI (the instructional component) is combined with CMI.

In a CMI environment, for example, the computer might make assignments, track student performance, and keep various administrative records. These administrative records might include a student's performance on various instructional exercises, the amount of time taken to complete an assignment, and even the specific time of day or night the student logged on. The time and effort saved by having course material and management functions handled by computer can be used by the instructor to work with students with special needs or instructional requirements.

At the same time, all students benefit by having the freedom to participate in computer-managed courses with greater flexibility. Often, arrangements can be made to complete course assignments during evenings, weekends, or whenever computer terminals are available. In many cases, it is possible to complete assignments from home through the use of modems linked to the students' personal computer.

Through CMI, the distant educator can provide geographically dispersed students with access to courses available to on-campus students in more traditional formats.

6.5.3 Computer-Mediated Education (CME).
Computer-mediated education (CME) describes computer applications that facilitate the delivery of instruction. Examples include electronic mail, fax, and real-time computer conferencing.

Electronic mail provides an easily accessible and interactive means for teacher-student and student-student interaction. A modem typically links computer terminals via phone lines. Messages are addressed to individual user identifications (IDs) or posted on electronic bulletin boards that are accessible to larger user groups. It is important to note, however, that instructional assignments submitted by electronic mail should be outlined prior to electronic mail distribution. This counteracts the tendency to compose and submit assignments without adequate planning and organization.

In addition to their role as a mail and messaging service, the systems can function as real-time computer conferencing tools in distance delivery courses.

Like electronic mail, computer conferencing provides a written form of communication and is relatively easy to use. Computer conferencing, however, provides real-time interaction by allowing participants to send and respond to messages simultaneously. This enhances interactive communication with more of the spontaneity present in "live" discussions (see Waggoner, 1992).

6.5.4 Computer-Based Multimedia (CBM). HyperCard, hypermedia, and a still-developing generation of powerful, sophisticated, and flexible computing tools have gained the attention of distance educators in recent years. The goal of computer-based multimedia is to integrate various voice, video, and computer technologies into a single, easily accessible delivery system.

An integrated computer-driven system of instructional delivery allows the instructional designer and faculty member to focus on content requirements and student needs in a relatively constraint-free technological environment. Instructional segments requiring motion, for example, use computer-converted film or video segments. Voice synthesis provides verbal interaction, while textual content is electronically transmitted in a student-controlled environment.

6.5.5 Instructional Computing Advantages.
- Computers can facilitate self-paced learning. In the CAI mode, for example, computers individualize learning, while giving immediate reinforcement and feedback (Verduin & Clark, 1991).
- Computers are becoming a multimedia tool. With integrated graphic, print, audio, and video capabilities, computers are beginning to effectively

link various technologies. Interactive video and CD-ROM technologies are being incorporated into computer-based instructional units, lessons, and learning environments.

- Computers are interactive. Microcomputer systems incorporating various software packages are extremely flexible and maximize learner control.
- Computer technology is rapidly advancing. Innovations are constantly emerging, while related costs drop. By understanding their present needs and future technical requirements, the cost conscious distance educator can effectively navigate the volatile computer market.
- Computers increase access. Local, regional, and national networks link resources and individuals, wherever they might be. In fact, some institutions offer complete undergraduate and graduate programs relying almost exclusively on computer-based resources.

6.5.6 Instructional Computing Limitations.

- Computer networks are costly to develop. Although individual computers are relatively inexpensive and the computer hardware and software market is very competitive, it is still costly to develop instructional networks as well as purchase the system software to run them.
- The technology is changing rapidly. Computer technology evolves so quickly that the distant educator focused on innovation—not meeting real needs—will constantly change equipment in an effort to keep pace with the "latest" technical advancements.
- Widespread computer illiteracy still exists. While computers have been widely used since the 1960s,

there are many who still refuse to acknowledge their role and potential importance. Even with today's latest generation of easy-to-use hardware and software, some educators remain hesitant to make use of computers in instructional settings.

Ironically, younger learners typically develop computing skills faster than adults, who must often overcome mental blocks before attaining computer literacy.

• Computers require a motivated learner. As with most forms of distance learning, students must be highly motivated and proficient in computer operation before they can successfully function in a computer-based distance learning environment.

6.6 Print Tools

No distance education teaching tool receives greater use and less attention than print. Print is the foundation of distance education and the basis from which all other delivery systems have evolved. The importance of print continues today, with the major distance teaching universities continuing to use print as a foundational element of their distance curriculums (Bates, 1982).

In fact, the first distance-delivered courses were offered by correspondence study, with print materials sent and returned to students by mail. As technological developments led to the use of radio, television, and audio courses, the role of print has actually increased in significance.

6.6.1 Print Advantages.

• *Spontaneous.* Print materials can be used in any setting without the need for sophisticated equipment and the concomitant time required to set up and master its operation.

- *Instructionally transparent.* The medium of delivery should enhance not compete with the content for the learner's attention. If the student reads well, the print medium is the most transparent instructional medium of all.
- *Non-threatening.* Reading is second nature to most students. As a result, they are easily able to focus on the content, without becoming mesmerized or frustrated by the process of reading itself.
- *Easy to use.* Given adequate light, print materials can be used any time and any place without the aid of supplemental resources such as electricity, viewing screens, and specially designed electronic classrooms. The portability of print is especially important for rural learners with limited access to sophisticated technology.
- *Easily reviewed and referenced.* Print materials are typically learner-controlled. As a result, the student rapidly moves through redundant sections, while focusing on areas demanding additional attention.
- *Cost-effective.* No instructional tool is less expensive to produce than print. In addition, facilities abound for the inexpensive duplication of these materials. Even if bound and printed in full color, with numerous illustrations, the associated costs of producing print materials are a fraction of electronic delivery systems.
- *Easily edited and revised.* In comparison to technically sophisticated electronic software, print is both easy and inexpensive to edit and revise.
- *Time-effective.* When instructional print materials are created, the developer's primary focus remains

on content concerns, not the technical requirements of the delivery system.

6.6.2 Print Limitations.

- *Limited view of reality.* Print, by its reliance on the
  written word, offers a vicarious view of reality.
  Despite the use of excellent sequential
  illustrations or photos, for example, it is impossible
  to adequately recreate motion in print.

  In an art class, for example, this can be used to
  instructional advantage by asking students to
  draw and compare illustrations of a person, place,
  or thing given the same narrative description.

- *Passive and self-directed.* Numerous studies have
  shown that high learner motivation is required to
  successfully complete print-based courses.

  To a certain extent, the passive nature of print can
  be offset by systematic instructional design that
  seeks to stimulate the passive learner. Still, it
  takes more motivation to read a book or work
  through a written exercise than it does to watch a
  television program or participate in an
  audioconference with an instructor encouraging
  student participation and response.

- *Feedback and interaction.* Without feedback and
  interaction, instruction suffers, regardless of the
  delivery system in use. By nature, print materials
  are passive and self-directed. Even with print
  materials incorporating feedback mechanisms and
  interactive exercises, it is easy for learners to skip
  to the answer section.

  To be most effective, print materials should
  creatively employ strategies for feedback and

interaction. Even when this is done, effective use requires a disciplined learner.

* *Dependent on reading skill.* Thanks to television, most students have developed fairly good viewing skills by age four. These same children, however, often fail to develop adequate reading skills by age 12.

Reading skills must often be improved. Lack of ability in this area cripples the effectiveness of even the most instructionally sound print material and must be overcome if print is to be used effectively.

6.6.3 Print Formats. Various print formats are available, including:

* *Textbooks.* As in traditionally delivered courses, textbooks are the basis and primary source of content for the majority of distance-delivered courses. While textbooks should always be critically reviewed before adoption, this is especially critical when the learner and instructor are not in daily contact. The textbook developer should be especially sensitive to using content examples that are relevant to the diverse audiences making use of them.

* *Study guides.* Typically, distance educators use study guides to reinforce the points made during class and through the use of other delivery systems. They will often include exercises, related readings, and additional resources available to the student.

* *Workbooks.* In a distance education context, workbooks are often used to provide course content in an interactive manner. A typical format might contain an overview, the content to be covered, one

or more exercises or case studies to elaborate the
points being made, and a quiz or test (with answer
key) for self-assessment. In addition, there is often
some form of feedback, remediation, or "branching"
loop to recycle students through the instruction as
needed.

• *Course syllabus.* A comprehensive and well-
planned course syllabus is the foundation of many
distance-delivered courses. It provides course goals
and objectives, performance expectations,
descriptions of assignments, related readings
(often by session), grading criteria, and a day-by-
day overview of the material to be covered.

• *Case studies.* If written imaginatively, case studies
are an extremely effective instructional tool. In
fact, case studies are often designed around the
limitations of print and intended to spark the
students' imaginations as they place themselves in
the particular case under consideration.

Many case studies present a content-based
scenario. They raise questions, pose alternative
solutions, and then branch students to different
sections of the text. There, the consequences of the
selected alternative are described.

**6.6.4 Improving Print's Instructional Effective-
ness.** There are numerous ways to improve the
effectiveness of print. Among them:

• *Organize content.* Prior to content development,
create an outline of the material to be covered.
Print materials are often too wordy because the
author is planning, organizing, and writing at the
same time. Instead, organize the content based on
the identified goals and objectives.

At this stage, sentence fragments, typographical errors, and incorrect punctuation are tolerable. Instead, the focus is on systematically and creatively ordering the flow of topics, not polishing a finished product. The end result will be a well-organized content outline from which the written content will easily flow.

- *Consistent format.* Learner anxiety with the unknown can be reduced through consistency in instructional presentation. Develop an effective format and organizational scheme and stick with it. Begin each section, for example, with a brief overview before moving to goals, objectives, content, a summary, case studies, a self-test, and a quiz.

- *Branching format.* Consider using a branching format for case studies and exercises. Based on student responses to questions and scenarios, refer them to different sections in the print resource.

- *Headings and subheadings.* Use an adequate number of headings and subheadings to visually guide your reader through the material.

- *Consistent punctuation and writing style.* Be consistent in capitalizing words, abbreviating expressions, indenting, and spacing. Find a good style guide and stick with it.

- *Keep your reader in mind.* As materials are developed, remember the target audience and make sure the writing style and word usage are appropriate.

- *Sentence and paragraph length.* Keep sentences and paragraphs reasonably short. It is better, for example, to use two short sentences rather than one that is long and circuitous.

- *Section summaries.* Make extensive use of summaries throughout the material to assist the reader in reviewing the material as it is covered.
- *Table of contents.* Make sure the table of contents provides sufficient detail, enabling the reader to quickly refer to the appropriate section.
- *Glossary of terms.* Incorporate a glossary containing definitions and an index of important terms.

6.7 In Summary

The key to effective distance education is focusing on the needs of the learners, the requirements of the content, and the constraints faced by the teacher before selecting a delivery system. Typically, this systematic approach will result in a mix of media, each serving a specific purpose. For example:

- A strong print component might be used to provide much of the basic instructional content in the form of a course text, as well as the syllabus and day-to-day schedule.
- Interactive audio or video conferencing could provide real time face-to-face (or voice-to-voice) interaction. This is also an excellent and cost-effective way to incorporate guest speakers and content experts.
- Computer conferencing or electronic mail could be used to send messages, mail, and other targeted communication to one or more class members.
- One-way television or interactive television could be used to present class lectures and related content requiring visualization.
- Audio graphics could be used to supplement audio-conferencing in providing a graphic component for visually oriented courses, such as math and science.

- Fax could be used to distribute assignments, last minute announcements, and to receive student assignments, especially when time is short and the mail service is slow and unreliable.

A variety of other distance delivery technologies are also available, including telephones, photocopy, audiotape recorders, and video cassette players/recorders.

Using this integrated approach, the educator's task is to carefully select among the technological options. The goal is to build a mix of instructional media, meeting the needs of the learner in a manner that is instructionally effective and financially prudent.

7.0

Strategies for Effective Teaching at a Distance: A Summary

7.1 Meeting Student Needs

To function effectively, students must quickly become comfortable and competent with the realities of teaching and learning at a distance. Efforts should be made to adapt the delivery system to better meet the needs of the students in terms of both content and preferred learning styles. Towards this end:

* Make learners aware of and comfortable with new patterns of communication to be used in the course.

* Develop an understanding of student backgrounds and experiences. Sharing the background and interest of the instructor is equally important.

* Be sensitive to different communication styles and varied cultural backgrounds. Remember, for example, that students may have different language skills and that humor is culturally specific and won't translate equally well to all students.

* Remember that students must take an active role in the distance-delivered course. They must assume greater responsibility for their own learning and

understand that more independent activity will be required.

• Assist students in becoming familiar and comfortable with the delivery technology, and prepare them to deal with the technical problems that will arise.

• Be sensitive to student needs in meeting standard university or school deadlines, despite the lag time often involved in mail delivery.

7.2 Course Planning and Organization

In developing or adapting distance-delivered instruction, the core content remains basically the same, although its presentation will require new strategies and additional preparation time. Consider the following:

• Before developing something new, review existing materials for content and presentation ideas.

• Incorporate a variety of appropriate media into course delivery plans. But, first, analyze the strengths and weaknesses of the delivery approaches under consideration, and refrain from using technology just because it is available.

• Demystify the distant teaching process by practicing with technological delivery systems prior to the start of class. Focus on distant teaching strategies, hands-on experience, behind-the-scenes technical operation, and post-class debriefings.

• Make sure each site is properly equipped with functional and accessible equipment. Provide a toll-free hotline for reporting problems.

• Set rules, guidelines, and standards for the course and uphold them.

- Have all materials on site before the course begins. Consider sending out materials and storing them with community-based elementary or secondary school personnel.
- Start off slowly with a manageable numbers of sites and students. The logistics of distant teaching increase exponentially with each additional site. Starting off slowly will enhance instructional effectiveness and increase both teacher and student comfort.

7.3 Teaching Strategies

As in all teaching, distance delivery confronts the instructor with numerous challenges and opportunities. To overcome the difficulties and capitalize on the opportunities, consider the following:

- Present overall course goals and objectives to students both verbally and in writing. Begin each class session with a review of what was covered previously as well as what will be covered in the current session.
- Develop strategies for student reinforcement, review, repetition, and remediation.
- Realistically assess how much content can be covered during each session. Presenting content at a distance is typically more time consuming than presenting the same content in a traditional classroom setting.
- Diversify and pace course activities and avoid long lectures. Intersperse content presentations with discussions and student-centered exercises.
- Be aware that members of the audience will have different learning styles. Some will learn more easily in group settings, while others will excel when working independently. Although the same is true in

traditional classroom settings, preferred student learning styles are more difficult to determine at a distance.

* Humanize the course by focusing on the students, not the delivery system.
* Provide a strong print component to supplement non-print materials.
* Use locally relevant case studies and examples as often as possible to help students understand and apply course content.
* Personalize instructor involvement, realizing that distant teaching does not replace the importance of face-to-face contact and small group interaction. If budget and time permit, teach at least one session from each site. Typically, the earlier in the course this is done, the better.
* Be concise. Use short, cohesive statements and ask direct questions.
* Vary the pace of content delivery. The pace should be slower for new material and faster for review.
* Relax. It will make both the instructor and students more comfortable.

7.4 Interaction and Feedback

Interaction and feedback are essential components of effective distance learning experiences. Interaction and feedback can take many forms, including individual phone calls, conference calls, computer conferencing, mail, and personal visits. Instructors can try the following:

* Contact each site (or student) every week if possible, especially early in the course. Take special note of

students who don't participate during the first session, and contact them individually after class.

- Return assignments without delay. Mail delivery adds days or even weeks from when an assignment is submitted to when instructor feedback is received. If practical, use fax or electronic mail for receiving and returning assignments.

- Make detailed and insightful comments on written assignments, referring to additional sources for supplementary information.

- Arrange telephone office hours using a toll-free number. Encourage students to call with questions, comments, and concerns. Early in the course, student-initiated calls should be mandatory in an effort to get them comfortable with the process. Since many students work during the day, consider posting evening office hours. If this is done, however, the specific times that evening calls are permitted should be stated.

- Use teaching strategies that encourage critical thinking and informed participation on the part of all learners. It may take time to eliminate poor communication patterns.

- Have students keep a weekly (or even daily) journal of their thoughts and ideas regarding the course content, as well as their individual progress and concerns. Have students submit journal entries several times during the class. Periodic journals are a good way of keeping students focused on the course, even if it doesn't meet weekly.

- Use pre-stamped and addressed postcards and out-of-class phone conferences for feedback regarding course content, relevancy, pace, delivery problems, and instructional concerns. Interest in receiving

feedback on course strengths and weaknesses should
be stressed.

• Use study questions, joint assignments, and community-based interviews to stimulate participation
by all sites and students.

• Meet students face to face whenever possible.
Getting to know students personally will facilitate
subsequent interaction and feedback. Encourage
them to stop and visit, whenever possible.

• Encourage students to query points they don't
understand. They are probably not alone in their
confusion.

• Politely but firmly discourage individual students or
sites from monopolizing class time.

• Arrange for students at individual sites to work
together on activities such as group presentations
and role playing.

• Have the facilitator provide guidance when students
are hesitant to ask questions or participate.

7.5 In Summary

At first glance, the task of developing or adapting a
course for distance delivery may appear intimidating or
at least foreign. Little may be known, for example,
about the students to be taught, the specific needs to be
addressed, and the technology to be used. Adding to
this uncertainty is the reality that faculty often feel
isolated in their efforts to prepare for this new teaching
experience.

By reducing the planning and teaching process into
logical and easily followed strategies, much of this
initial concern can be eliminated. In fact, many faculty
feel that the instructional strategies they employ at a
distance improve their face-to-face teaching as well.

8.0
The Future of Distance Education

8.1 Is Distance Education Here to Stay?

In recent years, distance education has become a popular catch phrase, generating interest among academicians and equipment vendors intrigued by the instructional and financial possibilities it offers.

However, it is important to remember that potential is one thing and substance is another. Regardless of the field or endeavor, potential without substance is short-lived. That is the problem confronted by educators when faced with promising or innovative instructional approaches used in such fields as distance education.

Educators often rely on an intuitive sense of potential instructional effectiveness and fail to ask basic questions to confirm or reject these intuitive assumptions. Subsequent efforts to reinforce intuition with hard data often fall short. While intuition can provide a glimpse at the potential benefits of distance education, focused effort, research, and the resolution of complex instructional questions will determine if the current interest in distance education is justified.

8.2 Improving Distance Education Research

Educators need to review existing distance education research while improving the quantity and quality of future research efforts (see Maddux, 1992).

While early studies and intuition suggest the importance of such variables as interaction, rapid feedback, and on-site facilitation in distance education contexts, more work is needed to answer a variety of focused questions, including:

- What are the specific types and benefits of student-to-student interaction?
- How important is rapid feedback, and what variables determine its effectiveness in distance education?
- What are the different roles and functions filled by on-site facilitators, and how can their impact be maximized?
- How critical is it to include locally relevant content examples, and how can this be more effectively accomplished?
- How can distance education more effectively meet the needs of students from widely diverse cultural backgrounds and varying educational experiences?
- Under what circumstances is distance education an appropriate (or inappropriate) method of instructional delivery?
- What role does cognitive style play in predicting student success in distance education, and are there valid ways of matching delivery methods to varied learning styles?
- What are the positive and negative effects of simultaneously teaching on-site and distant

students? Do distant learners get as much from the experience as their on-site counterparts?

- What factors determine when on-site and distant learners should be taught simultaneously or separately?

8.3 Learning from the Past

Although the technology of delivery has become more sophisticated in recent years, current distance education practices have evolved from earlier efforts in the field of correspondence study. In reviewing the literature of correspondence study, distance educators should find out:

- What research on the effectiveness of different approaches to correspondence study has been conducted, and how does it translate to the methods and technologies used today?
- What steps were taken to understand the wide-ranging audiences participating in these early correspondence study programs?
- What studies were conducted comparing the performance of home-based, independent study students with their in-class counterparts? What were the results? Are these results generalizable to today's distant learners?
- Are the strategies used by early distance educators to develop and deliver print-based courses still valid for the more technologically sophisticated courses of today? If so, in what ways? If not, why not?

8.4 Learning from Others

In the past 25 years, the distance education leadership has come from Australia, Europe, and Canada. In 1969, for example, the Open University was established in the United Kingdom, and in 1972, Canada's Athabasca University came into existence.

Both institutions provide an informative and exhaustive paper trail of benefit to distance educators in the United States. For example, in 1980 Athabasca University issued a report series detailing such topics as learner motivation factors (Coldeway, Spencer, & Stringer, 1980) and completion rates of distance education students receiving instruction via different delivery methods (Spencer, Peruniak, & Coldeway, 1980). In addition, Athabasca University publishes *Research in Distance Education*, a publication that shares the research spotlight with Pennsylvania State University's *American Journal of Distance Education*.

In reviewing international trends in the field, distance educators should determine:

• What similarities and differences exist among distance education students from culturally diverse countries?
• What course development models and evaluation strategies have gained international acceptance?
• What distance education management structures are in place in other countries and what can be gained by better understanding them?
• What levels and types of government support do distance education programs in other countries enjoy, in comparison to the United States?

8.5 Exploring Effective Evaluation Strategies

Traditional classroom instruction has been under scrutiny for years. Over time, a number of pencil-and-paper forced response methods have been developed for collecting information from learners. Still, educators need to evaluate the effectiveness of various forms of distance delivery evaluation (see Section 5.6). In doing so, a number of questions should be addressed, including:

- Under what circumstances and situations are qualitative as opposed to quantitative methods most useful in distance education?
- Under what conditions are qualitative evaluation results generalizable to other distance education settings?
- What quantitative and qualitative data collection and analysis methods are most appropriate, and how can they best be implemented?
- How can the rate of return for completed evaluation forms be improved?
√ • What questions need to be asked to better evaluate the effectiveness of distance education programs and technology?

8.6 Systematically Integrating Technology

Technical innovation continues at a pace that is difficult to measure or monitor. As a result, distance educators confront increasingly complex and sophisticated technical questions without adequate knowledge to allow systematic decision-making. One of two results is likely: either educators put off technological decisions for fear an updated version will come along, rendering their current technological approach outdated, or they blindly select technology, hoping for the best.

A better and more systematic approach to making technical decisions will result in the merging of less sophisticated but effective technology (audiotapes, video, and print) with more sophisticated delivery approaches using audioconferencing, audio graphics, interactive video, multimedia, fax, and electronic mail.

Distance educators faced with this process of technological selection and integration should address many issues, including:

* What content and learner variables determine the most appropriate delivery methods?
* What are the most critical learner and content decisions to be made before selecting appropriate instructional technology?
* What delivery options are currently available, and what related trends are developing?
* What cost and benefit factors should be addressed in selecting appropriate distance education technology?

8.7 Developing Responsive Academic Policy

Once the content is developed, the software has been field tested and revised, the hardware system is in place, and program implementation begins, many distance educators and administrators feel the major obstacles have been overcome.

This is far from the truth, especially if the distance-delivered course or program is effective and in demand on a system-wide basis. Under these circumstances, a plethora of challenging academic policy issues arise (Willis, 1989, 1991). These can be dealt with either reactively, or, better, proactively.

Many educational institutions spent the 1980s experimenting with various delivery methods and implementing these technical systems throughout their service areas. In contrast, the 1990s will be spent resolving the myriad academic policy issues and questions arising when wide-scale distance education is implemented. These include:

- How should distance education be administratively organized and managed?
- How should policy and procedural issues be resolved on a local campus and system-wide basis?
- What role should advisory committees play in identifying and resolving policy and procedural issues? How can their emphasis on academics, not technology, be ensured?
- How should the technical resources and infrastructure of educational institutions be deployed?
- How should distance delivery costs be shared by participating institutions?
- How and at what level should programs, services, and technical development be funded on a system-wide basis?
- What is the appropriate relationship between academic institutions and the telecommunication carriers providing technical services and support?
- How should academic programs with potential system-wide impact be identified, selected, and implemented?
- How should credit transfer issues be resolved?
- How should faculty development issues such as in-service training, instructional development support, and released time be addressed on a system-wide basis?
- How should promotion, tenure, and course load issues be resolved?
- How should support services be coordinated and funded on an individual institution and system-wide basis?

- How should courses offered system-wide be evaluated?
- How should the needs of distant learners be assessed?
- How should the qualifications of those teaching at a distance be assessed?
- Who should approve faculty qualifications and teaching assignments when courses are shared among institutions?
- How should inter-state agreements for program development and delivery be developed?

8.8 In Summary

While not exhaustive, the preceding review suggests a wide range of topics and issues to be explored by those involved in distance education. While it's true that distance education offers potential benefits, it is equally evident that insightful and substantive work in a number of related areas is required if the attention and interest it currently receives is to continue.

Glossary

Glossary of Selected Distance Education and Telecommunication Terms

Note: For a complete dictionary of telecommunication terms see Hansen (1991).

Asynchronous. A type of two-way communication that occurs with a time delay, allowing participants to respond at their own convenience.

Audio Bridge. Specialized equipment that permits several telephone lines to be joined together in a conference call.

Audioconference. An electronic meeting in which participants in different locations use telephones or audioconferencing equipment (e.g., microphones and convenors) to interactively communicate with each other in real time.

Audio Graphics. A sophisticated computer application relying on graphic computer interaction augmented by two-way, real-time audio communication. Audio, data, and graphics are shared over telephone lines, allowing users in different locations to simultaneously work on the same application.

Bandwidth. The frequency width needed to transmit a communication signal without excessive distortion. The more information contained in a signal, the more bandwidth it requires for distortion-free transmission.

Baud Rate. The transmission rate at which data flows between computers. It is synonymous with bits per second (bps).

Bulletin Board (computer-based). A personal computer with an auto-answer modem used to access a "host" computer for the purpose of reading and posting electronic messges.

C-Band. A type of satellite transmission with less path loss than other satellite standards such as Ku Band. C-Band, however, requires a relatively large antenna. C-Band frequencies are shared with terrestrial microwave transmissions, which can cause interference with weaker satellite signals in certain areas.

Central Processing Unit (CPU). A computer system's central processor. Contains main storage, arithmetic unit, and registers (Sippl, 1990).

Codec. Coding-decoding equipment used to convert and compress analog video signals into a digital format for transmission, then convert them back to analog signals upon reaching their destination.

Compressed Video. A digital transmission process used to transmit a video channel. While compressed video requires less bandwidth, signal quality is reduced. As a result, picture quality is generally not as good as full-motion, with quick motions often appearing somewhat blurred.

Distance Education. The organizational framework and process of providing instruction at a distance. Distance education takes place when a teacher and student(s) are physically separated, and technology (i.e., voice, video, data, or print) are used to bridge the instructional gap.

Distance Learning. The desired outcome of distance education, i.e., learning at a distance. See Distance Education.

Downlink. A dish-shaped antenna used to receive signals transmitted from a satellite.

Downloading. A procedure for transferring or retrieving a file from a distant computer and storing it on your own. Opposite of uploading.

Duplex Video. Two-way video communication capable of simultaneous origination and reception.

Earth Station. A ground-placed antenna used to transmit or receive signals to or from satellites, typically located in geostationary orbit.

Fax Machine (Facsimile). A photocopy device transmitting printed material to distant sites through the use of telephone lines.

Fiber Optic Cable. Bundled glass rods that are extremely thin and flexible and are capable of transmitting voice, video, and data signals in either analog or digital formats. This is accomplished with very little loss in signal quality.

Floppy Disk. A nonrigid magnetic disk on which data are stored.

Footprint. The area of the earth's surface that can receive the signal of a given satellite.

Full-Motion Video. Unlike compressed video signals (which tend to be blurry), full-motion video refers to high-quality signals, similar to what is received over a television set.

Geostationary Orbit. An earth orbit located directly above the equator, approximately 22,300 miles above the surface. Satellites in this orbit rotate at the same relative speed as the earth itself. This allows earth antennas to remain fixed.

Hard Drive (Hard Disk). A rigid nonremovable disk in a computer and the drive that houses it. Hard disks store much more data and access it much more quickly than floppy disks.

Instructional Development. The cyclical and systematic process of designing, developing, evaluating, and revising instruction.

Instructional Television Fixed Service (ITFS). A band of low-power microwave frequencies set aside by the Federal Communications Commission (FCC) exclusively for the transmission of educational programming, and licensed to public institutions. ITFS is typically used in urban areas and requires a specialized antenna. Receiving sites require a converter capable of changing signals to those used by a standard television set.

Ku-Band. A type of satellite transmission of a higher frequency than C-Band transmissions, and requiring smaller antennas.

Logging On. Connecting to a computer network, typically through the use of a personalized identification code.

Mainframe Computer. A large, relatively complex computer. Its capacity exceeds that of minicomputers and microcomputers.

Microcomputer. A computer with a microprocessor chip-based processing unit. Microcomputers are the original personal computers that many people use at home and at work.

Microwave. High-frequency radio waves used for point-to-point and omnidirectional communication of audio, data, and video signals. Microwave frequencies require direct line of sight to operate. Obstructions in the path usually distort or block the signal.

Minicomputer. A small digital computer typically relying on more than a single processor chip. A minicomputer is larger than a microcomputer but smaller than a mainframe.

Modem. Equipment that converts digital signals into analog signals for purpose of transmission. Modems are typically used to link computers via telephone lines. Short for modulator-demodulator.

Multiplex. The act of combining input signals from many sources onto a single communications path, or the use of a single path for transmitting signals from several sources (Sippl, 1990).

Network. A configuration of two or more computers linked to share information and resources.

Node. An origination or reception site.

One-Way Video/Two-Way Audio. An interactive conference, class, or meeting in which the distant participants view the conference leader through a video link. Two-way audioconferencing is used for real-time verbal interaction.

Originating Site. The site initiating the telecommunicated conference or meeting.

Real Time. An application in which information is received and immediately responded to.

Receiving Sites. All sites, other than the originating site, participating in a telecommunicated conference or meeting.

Satellite. An earth-orbiting device used for receiving and transmitting signals.

Simplex Video. One-way video communication capable of origination and reception, though not simultaneously.

Synchronous. A system in which regularly occuring events in timed intervals are kept in step using some form of electronic clocking mechanism.

Telecommunication. The process of transmitting or receiving information over a distance by any electrical or electromagnetic medium. Information may take the form of voice, video, or data.

Teleconferencing. Interactive communication among people at two or more locations using telecommunication. May involve audio, graphics, computer, or video communication.

Transponder. A single section of a satellite used to transmit and receive signals.

Two-Way Video/Two-Way Audio. Interactive video in which all sites are in visual contact with one another. Some form of audioconferencing is used for real-time verbal interaction.

Uplink. A satellite dish used to transmit an electronic signal up to a satellite transponder.

Uploading. The transfer of copies of a program or file from the user's own terminal to a remote data base or other computer. The reverse of downloading (Sippl, 1990).

Video Conference. A meeting, instructional session, or conversation between people at different locations relying on video technology as the primary communication link.

References

Bates, A. W. (1982). Trends in the use of audiovisual media. In J. S. Daniel, M. A. Stroud, & J. R. Thompson (Eds.), *Learning at a distance: A world perspective*. Edmonton, Alberta, Canada: International Council for Distance Education.

Batey, A., & Cowell, R. N. (1986). *Distance education: An overview*. Portland, OR: Northwest Regional Educational Laboratory. (ERIC Document Reproduction Service No. ED 278 519.)

Boone, M. E. (1984). Examining excellence: An analysis of facilitator behaviors in actual audio teleconferences. In *Teleconferencing and electronic communications* (3rd ed.) (pp. 218–222). Madison, WI: University of Wisconsin Extension, Center for Interactive Programs.

Boswell, J. J., Mocker, D. W., & Hamlin, W. C. (1968). Telelecture: An experiment in remote teaching. *Adult Leadership, 16*(9), 321–322.

Bronstein, R., Gill, J., & Koneman, E. (1982). *Teleconferencing: A practical guide to teaching by telephone*. Chicago: American Society of Clinical Pathologists Press.

Brookfield, S. D. (1990). *The skillful teacher: On technique, trust, and responsiveness in the classroom*. San Francisco: Jossey-Bass.

Centra, J. A. (1976). *Faculty development practices in U.S. colleges and universities.* Princeton, NJ: Educational Testing Service.

Christopher, G. R. (1982). The Air Force Institute of Technology: The Air Force reaches out through media: An update. In *Teleconferencing and Electronic Communications* (pp. 343–344). Madison, WI: University of Wisconsin–Extension, Center for Interactive Programs.

Chu, G., & Schramm, W. (1975). *Learning from television: What does the research say?* Stanford, CA: Stanford University Press. (ERIC Document Reproduction Service No. ED 014 900.)

Clark, R. E. (1985). Confounding in educational computing research. *Journal of Educational Computing Research, 1*(2), 137–147.

Coldeway, D. O., Spencer, R., & Stringer, M. (1980). *Factors effecting learner motivation in distance education: The interaction between learner attributes and learner course performance.* Project REDEAL, Research and Evaluation of Distance Education for the Adult Learner. Edmonton Alberta, Canada: Athabasca University.

Davis, D. J. (1984). Evaluation and comparison of teleconference training with face-to-face training and the effect on attitude and learning. *Dissertation Abstracts International, 46,* AAC85079.

Downing, D. E. (1984). *Survey on the uses of distance learning in the U.S.* Austin, TX: Southwest Educational Development Laboratory. (ERIC Document Reproduction Service No. ED 246 874.)

Educational Technology Publications. (1991). *Telecommunications for learning* (Educational Technology Anthology Series, Volume Three). Englewood Cliffs, NJ: Educational Technology Publications.

Eiserman, W. D., & Williams, D. D. (1987). *Statewide evaluation report on productivity project studies related to improved use of technology to extend education programs. Sub-report two: Distance education in elementary and secondary schools.* Logan, UT: Wasatch Institute for Research and Evaluation. (ERIC Document Reproduction Service No. ED 291 350.)

Forbes, N., Ashworth, C., Lonner, W., & Kasprzyk, D. (1984). *Television's effects on rural Alaska: Summary of final report.* Fairbanks, AK: University of Alaska Fairbanks, Center for Cross-Cultural Studies.

Gaff, J. G. (1975). *Toward faculty renewal.* San Francisco: Jossey-Bass.

Gilcher, K. W., & Johnstone, S. M. (1988). *A critical review of the use of audiographic conferencing systems by selected education institutions.* College Park, MD: University of Maryland, College Office of Instructional Communications.

Guba, E. G. (1978). Toward a methodology of naturalistic inquiry in educational evaluation. *CSE Monograph Series in Evaluation.* Los Angeles: Center for the Study of Evaluation, University of California.

Guba, E. G., & Lincoln, Y. S. (1981). *Effective evaluation: Improving the usefulness of evaluation results through responsive and naturalistic approaches.* San Francisco: Jossey-Bass.

Hansen, D. E. (1991). *Educational technology telecommunications dictionary with acronyms.* Englewood Cliffs, NJ: Educational Technology Publications.

Heinich, R., Molenda, M., & Russell, J. D. (1985). *Instructional media and the new technologies of instruction* (2nd ed.). New York: John Wiley.

Henderson, E. S., & Nathenson, M. B. (1984). *Independent learning in higher education.* Englewood Cliffs, NJ: Educational Technology Publications.

Holmberg, B. (1985). *Communication in distance study.* In *Status and trends of distance education* (pp. 87–100). Lund, Sweden: Lector Publishing.

Holmberg, B. (1990). *Theory and practice of distance education.* Boston: Routledge and Kegan.

Hoyt, D. P., & Frye, D. (1972). *The effectiveness of telecommunications as an educational delivery system.* Manhattan, KS: Kansas State University. (ERIC Document Reproduction Service No. ED 070 318.)

Kulik, C.-L. C., Kulik, J. A., & Schwalb, B. J. (1985). *The effectiveness of computer-based adult education.* Paper presented at the 69th annual meeting of the American Educational Research Association, Chicago, March 31–April 4. (ERIC Document Reproduction Service No. ED 263 888.)

Kurpius, D. J., & Christie, G. S. (1978). A systematic and collaborative approach to problem solving. In D. J. Kurpius (Ed.), *Learning: Making learning environments more effective* (pp. 13–16). Muncie, IN: Accelerated Development.

Lewis, R. J. (1985). *Instructional applications of information technologies: A survey of higher education in the west.* Boulder, CO: Western Interstate Commission for Higher Education.

Lochte, R. H. (1993). *Interactive television and instruction: A guide to technology, technique, facilities design, and classroom management.* Englewood Cliffs, NJ: Educational Technology Publications.

Macken, E. (1976). *Home-based education.* Washington, DC: U.S. Department of Health, Education, and Welfare.

Maddux, C. D. (1992). *Distance education: A selected bibliography.* Englewood Cliffs, NJ: Educational Technology Publications.

Moore, M. G., & Thompson, M. M. (1990). *The effects of distance learning: A summary of the literature.* University Park, PA: American Center for the Study of Distance Education. The Pennsylvania State University.

Nelson, P. (1985). *The effects of field independent-dependent cognitive style on achievement in a telecourse.* Unpublished doctoral dissertation, Brigham Young University, Provo, UT.

Ohler, J. (1988). A distance education chronology. *Online Journal of Distance Education and Communication, 1.*

Orlansky, S., & String, J. (1979). *Cost-effectiveness of computer-based education in military training.* Arlington, VA: Science, and Technical Divisions, Institute for Defense Analysis, IDA paper.

Purdy, L. (1978). *Telecourse students: How well do they learn?* Unpublished manuscript. San Diego, CA: University of California-San Diego. (ERIC Document Reproduction Service No. ED 154 851.)

Romiszowski, A. J. (1992). *Computer mediated communication: A selected bibliography.* Englewood Cliffs, NJ: Educational Technology Publications.

Showalter, R. G. (1983). *Speaker telephone continuing education for school personnel serving handicapped children: Final project report 1981–82.* Indianapolis, IN:

Indiana State Department of Public Instruction, Indianapolis Division of Special Education.

Sippl, C. J. (1990). *The new Webster's computer terms.* Costa Mesa, CA: Lexicon Publications.

Smeltzer, L. R. (1986). An analysis of receivers' reactions to electronically mediated communication. *The Journal of Business Communication, 23*(4), 37–54.

Spencer, R. E., Peruniak, G., & Coldeway, D. O. (1980). *A comparison between paced package and home study courses with respect to completion data. Project REDEAL, Research and Evaluation of Distance Education for the Adult Learner.* Edmonton, Alberta, Canada: Athabasca University.

Sponder, B. (1990). *Reaching the way-out student: A qualitative study of students in audioconference courses in western Alaska.* Unpublished doctoral dissertation, Utah State University, Logan.

Sponder, B. (1991). *Distance education in rural Alaska: An overview of teaching and learning practices in audioconference courses* (2nd ed.). Fairbanks, AK: University of Alaska Fairbanks, Center for Cross-Cultural Studies.

U.S. Congress, Office of Technology Assessment (1989). *Linking for learning: A new course for education.* Washington, DC: U.S. Government Printing Office, OTA-SET-0430.

Verduin, J. R., & Clark, T. A. (1991). *Distance education: The foundations of effective practice.* San Francisco: Jossey-Bass.

Waggoner, M. (1992). *Empowering networks: Computer conferencing in education.* Englewood Cliffs, NJ: Educational Technology Publications.

Whittington, N. (1987). Is instructional television education-ally effective? A research review. *American Journal of Distance Education, 1*(1), 47–57.

Willis, B. (1989). *Identifying and prioritizing distance education needs.* Anchorage, AK: University of Alaska System.

Willis, B. (1991). *Distance education policies and alternative actions.* Anchorage, AK: University of Alaska System.

Zigerell, J. (1984). *Distance education: An information age approach to adult education.* Columbus, OH: ERIC Clearinghouse on Adult, Career, and Vocational Education.

Index

A

adapting instruction 21, 38, 37–47, 73
administrator 5, 34, 39–40, 43
Alaska 80
Alberta Educational Communications Corporation 9
Athabasca University 9, 114
attrition 11, 20
audience 8, 18, 26, 53–62, 71, 100, 102, 107, 113
audio 66, 80–85, 115
  conferencing 17, 22, 73–74, 80–86, 115
  graphics 73, 83, 103, 115
Australia 9, 113

B

BC Knowledge Network 9
British influence 9
budget 32, 76, 108

C

CAI. *See* computer-assisted instruction
Canada 9, 113
CBM. *See* computer-based multimedia
Chicago TV College 15
CME. *See* computer-mediated education
CMI. *See* computer-managed instruction
Coast Community College District 15

About the Author

Barry Willis is Statewide Director of Distance Education for the University of Alaska System. He previously served as Associate Vice Chancellor for Distance Education and Academic Planning for the University of Alaska's Division of Community Colleges, Rural Education, and Extension. He moved to Alaska in 1981 as the Director of Instructional Development for the University's newly created telecommunication service.

Dr. Willis has taught at Boston University, the University of Alaska Fairbanks, Alaska Pacific University, and Utah State University. He has a doctorate in Instructional Systems Technology from Indiana University.